CAFE CLASSICS

THE AUSTRALIAN
Women's Weekly

contents

Simple, fast-cooking meals and snacks are the order of the day for us working women, mothers-on-the-go, and people who don't want to spend a lot of precious time in the kitchen (often, all one and the same person!). So, in this book, we've come up with a terrific cache of quick recipes, easily made with a modicum of fuss from ingredients found in most pantries. Why would you bother with packaged meals from the supermarket or takeaway when café food as good as this can be made in such short order?

Pamela Clark

Food Director

chocolate hazelnut croissants

PREPARATION TIME **15 MINUTES** COOKING TIME **15 MINUTES**

2 sheets ready-rolled puff pastry
⅓ cup (110g) Nutella
30g dark chocolate, grated finely
25g butter, melted
1 tablespoon icing sugar mixture

1 Preheat oven to hot. Lightly grease two oven trays.
2 Cut pastry sheets diagonally to make four triangles. Spread Nutella over triangles, leaving a 1cm border; sprinkle each evenly with chocolate.
3 Roll triangles, starting at one wide end; place 3cm apart on prepared trays with the tips tucked under and the ends slightly curved in to form crescent shape. Brush croissants with melted butter.
4 Bake, uncovered, in hot oven about 12 minutes or until croissants are browned lightly and cooked through. Sieve croissants with icing sugar; serve warm or at room temperature.

makes 8
per croissant 17.7g fat; 1153kJ (275 cal)

Spread the Nutella evenly over each of the triangles, leaving a 1cm border

Roll the triangles, starting at one wide end, to enclose the Nutella and chocolate filling

scrambled eggs with chorizo

PREPARATION TIME **5 MINUTES** COOKING TIME **10 MINUTES**

250g chorizo, sliced thickly
8 eggs
3/4 cup (180ml) cream
2 tablespoons coarsely
   chopped fresh chives
10g butter

1 Cook chorizo, in batches, on
   heated grill plate (or grill or
   barbecue) until browned both
   sides; cover to keep warm.
2 Break eggs into medium bowl,
   whisk lightly; whisk in cream and
   half of the chives.
3 Melt butter in medium frying pan
   over low heat; cook egg mixture,
   stirring gently constantly, until
   egg mixture just begins to set.
4 Serve scrambled eggs, sprinkled
   with remaining chives, and
   chorizo on slices of the toasted
   bread of your choice.

serves 4
per serving 49.6g fat;
2239kJ (535 cal)

caramelised banana and hazelnut waffles

PREPARATION TIME **10 MINUTES**   COOKING TIME **15 MINUTES**

4 packaged belgian-style waffles
40g butter
4 ripe bananas (800g),
  sliced thickly
2 tablespoons brown sugar
1/2 cup (75g) roasted hazelnuts,
  chopped coarsely
1/3 cup (80ml) maple syrup

1 Preheat oven to moderately slow.
2 Place waffles, in single layer, on
   oven tray; heat, uncovered, in
   moderately slow oven for about
   8 minutes.
3 Meanwhile, melt butter in
   medium frying pan; cook
   banana, stirring, about 2 minutes
   or until hot. Add sugar; cook,
   uncovered, over low heat, about
   2 minutes or until banana is
   caramelised lightly.
4 Divide waffles among serving
   plates; top with banana mixture,
   nuts and syrup.

serves 4
per serving 27.2g fat;
2283kJ (545 cal)

home-fried potatoes, chipolatas and tomatoes

PREPARATION TIME **10 MINUTES**   COOKING TIME **25 MINUTES**

400g new potatoes, sliced thinly
2 large tomatoes (500g)
1/2 cup (85g) polenta
1/3 cup (80ml) olive oil
12 chipolatas (360g)
1 large brown onion (200g),
   chopped coarsely
1/4 cup loosely packed fresh
   oregano leaves
1 tablespoon fresh
   rosemary leaves

1 Boil, steam or microwave potato until just tender; drain.
2 Meanwhile, cut tomatoes into four slices; coat one side of each slice with polenta. Heat 1 tablespoon of the oil in large frying pan; cook tomato slices, polenta-side up, until just browned. Turn; cook until just browned. Remove from pan; cover to keep warm.
3 Cook chipolatas, uncovered, in same cleaned pan until browned all over and cooked through. Remove from pan; cover to keep warm.
4 Heat remaining oil in same cleaned pan; cook potato, stirring, until browned lightly. Add onion; cook, stirring, until potato is crisp and onion softened. Stir in oregano and rosemary.
5 Divide potato, chipolatas and tomato among serving plates.

serves 4
per serving 39.7g fat;
2349kJ (561 cal)

buttermilk pancakes with glazed strawberries

PREPARATION TIME **15 MINUTES**   COOKING TIME **15 MINUTES**

4 eggs

2 tablespoons caster sugar

1½ cups (375ml) buttermilk

100g butter, melted

1½ cups (225g)
   self-raising flour

GLAZED STRAWBERRIES

⅓ cup (80ml) water

½ cup (170g) marmalade

1 tablespoon caster sugar

2 tablespoons lemon juice

250g strawberries, quartered

1   Beat eggs and sugar in small bowl with electric mixer until thick; stir in buttermilk and half of the butter.

2   Sift flour into large bowl; whisk egg mixture gradually into flour until batter is smooth.

3   Heat heavy-base medium frying pan; brush pan with a little of the remaining butter. Pour ¼ cup of the batter into pan; cook, uncovered, until bubbles appear on surface of pancake. Turn pancake; cook until browned. Remove from pan; cover to keep warm. Repeat with remaining butter and batter.

4   Serve pancakes with glazed strawberries.

   glazed strawberries Place the water, marmalade, sugar and juice in small saucepan; bring to a boil. Add strawberries, reduce heat; simmer, uncovered, about 2 minutes or until strawberries are hot.

serves 4

per serving 28.5g fat;
2810kJ (671 cal)

french toast with berry compôte

PREPARATION TIME **15 MINUTES** COOKING TIME **10 MINUTES**

4 eggs
$^1/_2$ cup (125ml) cream
$^1/_4$ cup (60ml) milk
1 teaspoon finely grated orange rind
1 teaspoon ground cinnamon
$^1/_4$ cup (85g) honey
100g butter, melted
8 thick slices sourdough bread (320g)
$^1/_4$ cup (40g) icing sugar mixture
BERRY COMPOTE
1 teaspoon arrowroot
$^1/_3$ cup (80ml) water
2 cups (300g) frozen mixed berries
2 tablespoons caster sugar
1 tablespoon finely grated orange rind

1 Break eggs into medium bowl, whisk lightly; whisk in cream, milk, rind, cinnamon and honey.
2 Heat about a quarter of the butter in medium frying pan. Dip two bread slices into egg mixture, one at a time; cook, uncovered, until browned both sides. Remove both slices of French toast from pan; cover to keep warm. Repeat with remaining butter, bread slices and egg mixture.
3 Sieve French toast with icing sugar; serve with warm berry compôte.
   berry compôte Blend arrowroot with the water in small saucepan until smooth; add remaining ingredients. Cook until mixture almost boils and thickens slightly.

serves 4
per serving 42.4g fat; 3154kJ (753 cal)
serving suggestion Serve with freshly whipped cream.

triple-cheese muffins

PREPARATION TIME **10 MINUTES** COOKING TIME **20 MINUTES**

1 cup (150g) self-raising flour
$1/2$ teaspoon bicarbonate
   of soda
$1/4$ teaspoon cayenne pepper
2 eggs
$1 1/4$ cups (310ml) milk
20g butter, melted
4 green onions, chopped finely
2 tablespoons finely grated
   mozzarella cheese
2 tablespoons finely grated
   parmesan cheese
2 tablespoons finely grated
   cheddar cheese

1 Preheat oven to hot. Lightly
   grease eight holes of 12-hole
   ($1/3$ cup/80ml) muffin pan.
2 Combine flour, soda and
   cayenne in medium bowl. Break
   eggs in small bowl, whisk lightly;
   whisk in milk, butter and onion
   until combined. Pour egg mixture
   into flour mixture; whisk until
   batter is smooth. Divide half
   of the batter among prepared
   holes; top with combined
   cheeses then remaining batter.
3 Bake, uncovered, in hot oven
   about 20 minutes or until muffins
   are well risen.

serves 4
per serving 15.1g fat;
1334kJ (319 cal)

pancetta and eggs

PREPARATION TIME **10 MINUTES**   COOKING TIME **10 MINUTES**

8 slices pancetta (120g)
2 green onions,
    chopped coarsely
4 eggs
4 thick slices white bread

1 Preheat oven to moderately hot.
   Grease four holes of 12-hole
   (1/3 cup/80ml) muffin pan.
2 Line each of the prepared holes
   with 2 slices of the pancetta,
   overlapping to form cup shape.
   Divide onion among pancetta
   cups; break one egg into each
   pancetta cup.
3 Bake, uncovered, in moderately
   hot oven about 10 minutes or
   until eggs are just cooked and
   pancetta is crisp around edges.
   Remove from pan carefully.
   Serve on toasted bread.

serves 4
per serving 10.4g fat;
965kJ (231 cal)

smoked salmon omelette

PREPARATION TIME **10 MINUTES**   COOKING TIME **15 MINUTES**

6 eggs
$2/3$ cup (160ml) cream
1 tablespoon warm water
$2/3$ cup (160g) sour cream
2 tablespoons coarsely
   chopped fresh dill
1 tablespoon lemon juice
220g smoked salmon
30g baby rocket leaves

1 Break eggs into medium bowl,
   whisk lightly; whisk in cream.
2 Pour $1/4$ of the egg and cream
   mixture into heated lightly oiled
   22cm non-stick frying pan; cook
   over medium heat, tilting pan,
   until omelette is almost set. Run
   spatula around edge of pan to
   loosen omelette, turn onto plate;
   cover to keep warm. Repeat
   process with remaining egg
   mixture to make 4 omelettes.
3 Combine the water with sour
   cream, dill and juice in small
   bowl. Fold omelettes into
   quarters; place on serving plates.
   Top each with equal amounts of
   the salmon, sour cream mixture
   and rocket.

serves 4
per serving 43.8g fat;
2089kJ (499 cal)

fruit scrolls with spiced yogurt

PREPARATION TIME **10 MINUTES**   COOKING TIME **25 MINUTES**

40g butter
1/4 teaspoon ground nutmeg
1 1/2 tablespoons brown sugar
1 tablespoon ground cinnamon
1 small apple (130g), peeled,
    cored, grated coarsely
1/3 cup (50g) finely chopped
    dried apricots
1/2 cup (125ml) orange juice
1 sheet ready-rolled puff pastry
1/2 cup (140g) plain yogurt
1 tablespoon honey

1 Preheat oven to moderately hot.
   Lightly grease oven tray.
2 Melt half of the butter in small
   saucepan; add nutmeg, sugar
   and half of the cinnamon. Cook,
   stirring, over low heat, until sugar
   dissolves. Stir in apple, apricot
   and half of the juice; bring to
   a boil. Reduce heat; simmer,
   uncovered, 2 minutes. Remove
   from heat; stir in remaining juice.
3 Spread fruit mixture over pastry
   sheet; roll into log. Cut log into
   quarters; place on prepared tray,
   5cm apart, brush with remaining
   melted butter.
4 Bake, uncovered, in moderately
   hot oven about 20 minutes or
   until scrolls are cooked through.
5 Meanwhile, combine yogurt,
   honey and remaining cinnamon
   in small bowl. Serve hot scrolls
   with spiced yogurt dusted with
   sifted icing sugar, if desired.

serves 4
per serving 19.2g fat;
1442kJ (344 cal)

baked eggs with prosciutto and brie

PREPARATION TIME 10 MINUTES   COOKING TIME 15 MINUTES

1 tablespoon olive oil
100g prosciutto, chopped finely
100g button mushrooms,
   chopped finely
4 green onions, chopped finely
100g slightly underripe brie
   cheese, chopped coarsely
8 eggs

1 Preheat oven to moderately hot. Grease four ¾-cup (180ml) shallow ovenproof dishes.

2 Heat oil in medium frying pan; cook prosciutto and mushrooms, stirring, until mushrooms soften. Add onion; cook, stirring, until onion softens. Remove pan from heat; stir in half of the cheese.

3 Divide prosciutto mixture among dishes; break two eggs into each dish. Bake, uncovered, in moderately hot oven 5 minutes. Sprinkle remaining cheese over eggs; bake, uncovered, in hot oven about 5 minutes or until eggs set and cheese melts. Serve immediately with freshly ground black pepper, if desired.

serves 4
per serving 23.9g fat;
1307kJ (312 cal)

honey-roasted muesli

PREPARATION TIME **10 MINUTES**   COOKING TIME **15 MINUTES**

3/4 cup (60g) rolled oats
1/2 cup (55g) rolled rye
1/2 cup (55g) rolled rice
1/4 cup (15g) unprocessed
    wheat bran
1/2 cup (175g) honey
1 tablespoon vegetable oil
1/3 cup (40g) coarsely
    chopped walnuts
1/4 cup (40g) pepitas
1 teaspoon ground cinnamon
1/3 cup (50g) coarsely chopped
    dried apricots
1/3 cup (30g) coarsely chopped
    dried apples
1/4 cup (40g) raisins

1 Preheat oven to moderate.
2 Combine oats, rye, rice and bran
   in medium baking dish; drizzle
   evenly with honey and oil. Roast,
   uncovered, in moderate oven
   5 minutes.
3 Stir ingredients together in dish;
   roast, uncovered, 10 minutes.
4 Remove from oven; stir in
   remaining ingredients. Serve with
   milk or yogurt.

serves 4
per serving 18.1g fat;
2218kJ (530 cal)

tip You can double or triple the quantity of the ingredients and store the
muesli in an airtight container in the refrigerator for up to 3 months.
serving suggestion Top your muesli with fresh seasonal fruit.

denver omelette

PREPARATION TIME **10 MINUTES**   COOKING TIME **15 MINUTES**

10 eggs
1/3 cup (80g) sour cream
2 red thai chillies, seeded, chopped finely
2 teaspoons vegetable oil
3 green onions, sliced thinly
1 medium green capsicum (200g), chopped finely
100g leg ham, chopped finely
2 small tomatoes (260g), seeded, chopped finely
1/2 cup (60g) coarsely grated cheddar cheese

1 Break eggs in large bowl, whisk lightly; whisk in sour cream and chilli.
2 Heat oil in large non-stick frying pan; cook onion and capsicum, stirring, until onion softens. Place onion mixture in medium bowl with ham, tomato and cheese; toss to combine.
3 Pour 1/2 cup of the egg mixture into same lightly oiled frying pan; cook, tilting pan, over low heat until almost set. Sprinkle about 1/3 cup of the filling over half of the omelette; using spatula, fold omelette over to completely cover the filling.
4 Pour 1/4 cup of the egg mixture into empty half of pan; cook over low heat until almost set. Sprinkle about 1/3 cup of the filling over folded omelette, fold omelette over top of first omelette to cover filling. Repeat twice more, using 1/4 cup of the egg mixture each time, to form one large layered omelette. Carefully slide omelette onto plate; cover to keep warm.
5 Repeat steps 3 and 4 to make second omelette, using remaining egg and filling. Cut each denver omelette in half.

serves 4
per serving 29.5g fat; 1604kJ (383 cal)

Pour another 1/4 cup of the egg mixture into the empty half of the frying pan

Fold the omelette over the top of the first omelette to completely cover the filling

prosciutto and fontina croissants

PREPARATION TIME 10 MINUTES COOKING TIME 10 MINUTES

4 croissants
2 teaspoons olive oil
8 slices prosciutto (120g)
1/2 cup (50g) coarsely grated
   fontina cheese
100g semi-dried tomatoes,
   drained, sliced thinly
30g baby rocket

1 Preheat oven to moderately slow.
2 Split croissants in half horizontally,
   without separating; place on
   oven tray. Heat, uncovered, in
   moderately slow oven about
   5 minutes.
3 Meanwhile, heat oil in small
   frying pan; cook prosciutto
   about 5 minutes or until crisp.
   Drain on absorbent paper.
4 Place equal amounts of
   cheese inside croissants; cook,
   uncovered, in moderately slow
   oven about 5 minutes or until
   cheese melts. Fill croissants with
   prosciutto, tomato and rocket.

serves 4
per serving 25.7g fat;
1853kJ (443 cal)

corn fritters

PREPARATION TIME **5 MINUTES (PLUS STANDING TIME)** COOKING TIME **15 MINUTES**

1 cup (250ml) boiling water
1 cup (170g) polenta
1 teaspoon salt
1 egg, beaten lightly
1/2 cup (125ml) milk
40g butter, melted
1/2 cup (75g) self-raising flour
125g can corn kernels, drained
1/2 cup (60g) coarsely grated
    cheddar cheese
2/3 cup (170g) bottled chunky
    tomato salsa

1 Combine the water, polenta and
   salt in medium heatproof bowl;
   cover, stand 10 minutes.
2 Stir egg, milk and butter into
   polenta mixture, then add flour,
   corn and cheese; stir until batter
   is well combined.
3 Pour 1/4 cup of the batter into
   heated large lightly greased
   non-stick frying pan; using
   spatula, spread batter to shape
   into a round. Cook about
   2 minutes each side or until
   fritter is lightly browned and
   cooked through, remove from
   pan; cover to keep warm.
   Repeat with remaining batter.
4 Serve fritters with salsa.

serves 4
per serving 17.2g fat;
1732kJ (414 cal)

baked ricottas with roasted tomatoes

PREPARATION TIME 10 MINUTES COOKING TIME 25 MINUTES

2 tablespoons olive oil
2 cloves garlic, crushed
1/4 cup (40g) pine nuts
150g baby spinach leaves, chopped coarsely
2 medium tomatoes (380g)
400g ricotta cheese
2 eggs, beaten lightly
2/3 cup (50g) finely grated parmesan cheese
2 tablespoons finely chopped fresh chives

1 Preheat oven to hot. Grease four holes of 6-hole texas (3/4 cup/180ml) muffin pan.
2 Heat half of the oil in medium frying pan, cook garlic and nuts over low heat, stirring constantly, until nuts start to brown lightly. Add spinach; cook, covered, about 2 minutes or until spinach wilts. Cook, uncovered, about 2 minutes or until liquid evaporates. Remove from heat.
3 Cut each tomato into eight wedges; place in medium baking dish, drizzle with remaining oil. Roast, uncovered, in hot oven 20 minutes.
4 Meanwhile, combine ricotta, eggs, parmesan and chives in large bowl with spinach mixture. Divide mixture among prepared holes.
5 Bake, uncovered, in hot oven about 20 minutes or until ricottas are firm. Serve baked ricottas with roasted tomatoes.

serves 4
per serving 34.3g fat; 1711kJ (409 cal)

caramelised onion and red lentil dip

PREPARATION TIME 10 MINUTES   COOKING TIME 15 MINUTES

3/4 cup (150g) red lentils
2 cups (500ml) boiling water
2 cloves garlic, quartered
1 medium potato (200g),
   chopped coarsely
1/4 cup (60ml) olive oil
2 medium brown onions (300g),
   sliced thinly
1/2 teaspoon ground cumin
1 teaspoon ground coriander
1/4 teaspoon sweet paprika
2 tablespoons lemon juice

1 Combine lentils, the water,
   garlic and potato in medium
   saucepan; bring to a boil.
   Reduce heat; simmer, uncovered,
   about 15 minutes or until lentils
   soften, stirring occasionally.
2 Meanwhile, heat 2 tablespoons
   of the oil in medium frying
   pan; cook onion, stirring
   occasionally, about 8 minutes
   or until caramelised. Remove
   2 tablespoons of the onion from
   pan; reserve. Add spices to
   pan; cook, stirring, until fragrant.
   Remove from heat; stir in juice.
3 Blend or process lentil mixture
   and onion with remaining oil until
   dip is smooth. Top with reserved
   onion; serve with toasted pide or
   pitta crisps, if desired.

makes 2 1/2 cups
per tablespoon 2g fat;
153kJ (37 cal)

poached eggs with burned sage butter and asparagus

PREPARATION TIME **10 MINUTES** COOKING TIME **10 MINUTES**

80g butter
12 fresh sage leaves
4 eggs
200g asparagus, trimmed
4 english muffins
40g shaved parmesan cheese

1 Melt butter in small saucepan; cook sage, stirring, about 3 minutes or until butter changes colour to deep brown. Remove from heat; cover to keep warm.

2 Half-fill a shallow frying pan with water; bring to a boil. One at a time, break eggs into cup, then slide into pan. When all eggs are in pan, allow water to return to a boil. Cover pan, turn off heat; stand about 4 minutes or until a light film of egg white sets over yolks. One at a time, remove eggs, using egg slide, and place on absorbent-paper-lined saucer to blot up poaching liquid.

3 Meanwhile, boil, steam or microwave asparagus until tender. Drain; cover to keep warm. Split muffins; toast cut-side.

4 Place bottom halves of muffins on serving plates; top each with equal amounts of asparagus, an egg, 1 tablespoon of sage butter, and cheese. Serve with remaining muffin halves.

serves 4
per serving 25.8g fat; 1664kJ (398 cal)
tip When poaching the eggs, cover the frying pan with a glass lid so you can keep an eye on the poaching process. Don't lift the lid during poaching as the steam helps set the eggs.

chicken tandoori pockets with raita

PREPARATION TIME 10 MINUTES   COOKING TIME 10 MINUTES

Packages of large flour tortillas (sometimes labelled burrito tortillas) are an easy alternative to making your own authentic chapati or roti.

1 tablespoon lime juice
⅓ cup (100g) tandoori paste
¼ cup (70g) yogurt
400g chicken tenderloins
8 large flour tortillas
60g snow pea tendrils
RAITA
1 cup (280g) yogurt
1 lebanese cucumber (130g), halved, seeded, chopped finely
1 tablespoon finely chopped fresh mint

1 Combine juice, paste and yogurt in medium bowl; add chicken, toss to coat chicken in marinade.
2 Cook chicken, in batches, on heated oiled grill plate (or grill or barbecue) until cooked through. Stand 5 minutes; slice thickly.
3 Meanwhile, heat tortillas according to manufacturer's instructions.
4 Place equal amounts of each of the chicken, tendrils and raita on a quarter section of each tortilla; fold tortilla in half and then in half again to enclose filling and form triangle-shaped pockets.
raita Combine ingredients in small bowl.

makes 8
per pocket 8.8g fat; 1003kJ (240 cal)

Place equal amounts of the chicken, tendrils and raita on a quarter section of each tortilla

Fold tortilla in half and then in half again to form a triangle-shaped pocket

sweet potato soup

PREPARATION TIME **15 MINUTES** COOKING TIME **20 MINUTES**

25g butter

1 medium onion (150g),
   chopped coarsely

2 cloves garlic, quartered

2 bacon rashers (140g),
   chopped coarsely

1/2 cup (125ml) dry white wine

2 large potatoes (600g),
   chopped coarsely

3 small kumara (750g),
   chopped coarsely

2 cups (500ml) water

3 cups (750ml) chicken stock

1/4 cup (60ml) cream

2 teaspoons finely chopped
   fresh rosemary

1 Melt butter in large saucepan;
   cook onion, garlic and bacon,
   stirring, until onion softens. Add
   wine, potato and kumara; bring
   to a boil. Reduce heat; simmer,
   stirring, 2 minutes.

2 Add the water and stock; return
   soup to a boil. Reduce heat;
   simmer, covered, 15 minutes or
   until vegetables soften.

3 Blend or process soup mixture,
   in batches, until smooth. Return
   soup to pan; add cream and
   rosemary, reheat soup. Serve
   sprinkled with more fresh
   rosemary, if desired.

serves 4
per serving 15.9g fat;
1695kJ (405 cal)
serving suggestion Serve with
toasted olive foccacia.

cheesy chips topped with bacon and sour cream

PREPARATION TIME **10 MINUTES** COOKING TIME **25 MINUTES**

1kg frozen potato chips
1 tablespoon vegetable oil
1 clove garlic, crushed
6 bacon rashers (420g),
   sliced thinly
1/2 cup (120g) sour cream
1 tablespoon finely chopped
   fresh chives
1 red thai chilli, seeded,
   chopped finely
11/2 cups (180g) coarsely grated
   cheddar cheese

1 Preheat oven to moderately hot.
   Lightly grease oven tray.
2 Place chips, in single layer, on
   prepared tray. Cook, uncovered,
   in moderately hot oven about
   20 minutes or until brown.
3 Meanwhile, heat oil in medium
   frying pan; cook garlic and
   bacon, stirring, until bacon is
   crisp. Drain on absorbent paper.
4 Combine sour cream, chives and
   chilli in small bowl. Place chips
   on ovenproof serving platter.
   Sprinkle with bacon mixture and
   cheese; cook, uncovered, in
   moderately hot oven about
   5 minutes or until cheese melts.
5 Serve chips topped with sour
   cream mixture.

serves 4
per serving 61.2g fat;
4993kJ (1193 cal)

chicken chilli pizza

PREPARATION TIME **10 MINUTES**   COOKING TIME **20 MINUTES**

You need about half of a large barbecued chicken for this recipe.

4 x 125g pizza bases
2 tablespoons tomato paste
1 tablespoon barbecue sauce
1½ teaspoons sambal oelek
1 clove garlic, crushed
1 cup (170g) coarsely chopped
 cooked chicken
100g button mushrooms,
 sliced thickly
1 small tomato (130g), halved,
 sliced thinly
1½ cups (150g) coarsely
 grated pizza cheese
2 teaspoons fresh thyme leaves

1 Preheat oven to hot. Place pizza
   bases on oven tray. Combine
   paste, sauce, sambal and garlic
   in small bowl; spread evenly
   over bases. Divide chicken,
   mushrooms, tomato and cheese
   among bases.
2 Cook, uncovered, in hot oven
   about 20 minutes or until pizza
   bases are crisp. Top with thyme.

serves 4
per serving 15.4g fat;
2289kJ (547 cal)

teriyaki rice paper rolls

PREPARATION TIME **30 MINUTES**

You need about half of a large barbecued chicken for this recipe.

1 cup (160g) shredded
    cooked chicken
1 small carrot (70g),
    coarsely grated
1 small red capsicum (150g),
    sliced thinly
100g shiitake mushrooms,
    sliced thinly
50g snow pea tendrils
2 tablespoons coarsely
    chopped fresh coriander
2 tablespoons teriyaki sauce
1 tablespoon sweet chilli sauce
12 x 22cm rice paper rounds

1 Combine chicken, carrot,
   capsicum, mushrooms, tendrils,
   coriander and sauces in large
   bowl; mix gently.
2 Place one sheet of rice paper in
   medium bowl of warm water until
   just softened; lift sheet carefully
   from water, place on board,
   covered with a tea towel.
3 Place some of the filling in the
   centre of sheet; fold in sides, roll
   top to bottom to enclose filling.
   Repeat with remaining rice paper
   sheets and filling.

serves 4
per serving 2.6g fat;
791kJ (189 cal)
serving suggestion Serve with
sweet chilli sauce or soy sauce.

suppli al telefono

PREPARATION TIME 15 MINUTES   COOKING TIME 15 MINUTES

This delicious snack from Italy originally got its name from the melted mozzarella "strings" that resemble telephone wires when one of these croquettes is split open and pulled apart. You need to cook about 1/3 cup of rice for this recipe.

1 tablespoon olive oil
1/3 cup (40g) frozen peas
2 cloves garlic, crushed
1 cup cooked medium-grain white rice
1/3 cup (25g) finely grated parmesan cheese
1 egg, beaten lightly
1 tablespoon coarsely chopped fresh oregano
40g mozzarella cheese
1/2 cup (35g) stale breadcrumbs
vegetable oil, for deep-frying

1   Heat olive oil in large frying pan; cook peas and garlic until peas are just tender and garlic is fragrant.
2   Combine pea mixture in medium bowl with rice, parmesan, egg and oregano. Using hands, shape rice mixture into eight balls.
3   Cut mozzarella into eight cubes. Press a hole into the middle of each ball; insert one piece of the mozzarella, then re-mould rice to cover hole. Roll balls in breadcrumbs to coat all over.
4   Heat vegetable oil in large saucepan; deep-fry balls, in batches, until lightly browned and heated through.

makes 8
per ball 9.9g fat; 621kJ (148 cal)
tip   Leftover bolognese sauce can be used as a filling for suppli instead of the peas and cheese in this recipe.

potato wedges with sloppy joe topping

PREPARATION TIME 10 MINUTES COOKING TIME **30 MINUTES**

4 medium potatoes (800g)
2 tablespoons olive oil
1 clove garlic, crushed
1 large brown onion (200g),
    chopped finely
1 small green capsicum (150g),
    chopped finely
1 trimmed celery stick (75g),
    chopped finely
750g beef mince
2 tablespoons mild
    american mustard
2 tablespoons cider vinegar
1 cup (250ml) tomato sauce
½ cup (60g) coarsely grated
    cheddar cheese
2 green onions, sliced thinly

1 Preheat oven to hot.
2 Cut each potato into eight
    wedges; place in large shallow
    baking dish, drizzle with half of
    the oil.
3 Roast, uncovered, in hot oven
    about 30 minutes or until
    wedges are tender.
4 Meanwhile, heat remaining oil
    in large frying pan; cook garlic,
    brown onion, capsicum and
    celery, stirring, until vegetables
    soften. Add mince; cook, stirring,
    until changed in colour. Stir in
    mustard, vinegar and sauce;
    bring to a boil. Reduce heat; cook,
    stirring, until sloppy joe is cooked
    through and slightly thickened.
5 Serve wedges topped with
    sloppy joe mixture; sprinkle with
    cheese and green onion.

serves 4
per serving 28.9g fat;
2707kJ (647 cal)

mediterranean vegetables and haloumi bruschetta

PREPARATION TIME **15 MINUTES** COOKING TIME **10 MINUTES**

1 small french breadstick
1 tablespoon olive oil
1 small eggplant (230g),
    sliced thinly
200g haloumi cheese,
    sliced thinly
2 tablespoons plain flour
2 medium egg tomatoes (150g),
    sliced thinly
2 tablespoons fresh baby
    basil leaves
1 tablespoon baby capers,
    rinsed, drained

1 Preheat oven to hot.
2 Cut bread, on an angle, into
   eight slices; brush both sides
   with half of the oil, place on oven
   tray. Toast, uncovered, in hot
   oven about 5 minutes.
3 Meanwhile, cook eggplant on
   heated oiled grill plate (or grill or
   barbecue) until just tender.
4 Coat haloumi in flour; cook on
   heated oiled grill plate (or grill or
   barbecue) until browned lightly.
5 Divide eggplant, haloumi,
   tomatoes, basil and capers
   evenly among bruschetta. Drizzle
   with remaining oil.

serves 4
per serving 14.8g fat;
1277kJ (305 cal)

leek and fetta triangles

PREPARATION TIME 15 MINUTES   COOKING TIME 15 MINUTES

100g butter
2 cloves garlic, crushed
2 medium leeks (700g),
   sliced thinly
1 tablespoon caraway seeds
150g fetta cheese,
   chopped coarsely
1/3 cup (40g) coarsely grated
   cheddar cheese
4 sheets fillo pastry
2 teaspoons sesame seeds

1 Heat half of the butter in large
   frying pan; cook garlic and leek,
   stirring occasionally, until leek
   softens. Stir in caraway seeds;
   cook, stirring, 2 minutes.
2 Combine leek mixture in medium
   bowl with fetta and cheddar.
   Preheat oven to moderately hot.
   Lightly oil oven tray.
3 Melt remaining butter in small
   saucepan. Brush one sheet of
   the fillo lightly with butter; fold in
   half lengthways. Place 1/4 of the
   leek mixture at bottom of one
   narrow edge of fillo, leaving a
   1cm border. Fold opposite corner
   of fillo diagonally across the
   filling to form a triangle; continue
   folding to end of fillo, retaining
   triangular shape. Place on
   prepared tray, seam-side down;
   repeat with remaining ingredients
   to make four triangles in total.
4 Brush triangles with butter;
   sprinkle with sesame seeds.
   Bake, uncovered, in moderately
   hot oven about 10 minutes or
   until browned lightly.

serves 4
per serving 34.4g fat;
1711kJ (409 cal)
serving suggestion Serve with
a mixed leaf and tomato salad.

pizza supreme jaffle

PREPARATION TIME **10 MINUTES** COOKING TIME **10 MINUTES**

1 tablespoon olive oil
2 cloves garlic, crushed
1 small red onion (100g),
  sliced thinly
1 small green capsicum (150g),
  sliced thinly
50g swiss brown mushrooms,
  sliced thinly
1 long loaf pide
1/4 cup (70g) tomato paste
120g hot salami, sliced thinly
80g marinated artichoke hearts,
  drained, sliced thinly
100g bocconcini, sliced thickly

1 Heat oil in large frying pan; cook
  garlic and onion, stirring, until
  onion softens. Add capsicum
  and mushrooms; cook, stirring,
  until mushrooms soften.
2 Preheat sandwich press or
  jaffle maker. Cut bread
  crossways into four pieces;
  split each piece horizontally.
3 Spread paste evenly over four
  pieces of bread, then top with
  equal amounts of vegetable
  mixture, salami, artichoke and
  cheese. Top with remaining bread.
4 Toast sandwiches in heated
  sandwich press.

serves 4
per serving 27.9g fat;
2728kJ (652 cal)
tip If you do not have a sandwich
press or jaffle maker, you can
make these sandwiches in either
a frying pan or your oven.

chilli and garlic spaghettini with breadcrumbs

PREPARATION TIME **10 MINUTES**   COOKING TIME **10 MINUTES**

375g spaghettini
1/3 cup (80ml) olive oil
50g butter
4 cloves garlic, crushed
4 red thai chillies, seeded,
  chopped finely
2 cups (140g) stale
  breadcrumbs
1/2 cup coarsely chopped fresh
  flat-leaf parsley
2 teaspoons finely grated
  lemon rind

1 Cook pasta in large saucepan
   of boiling water, uncovered, until
   just tender.
2 Meanwhile, heat half of the oil in
   large frying pan with butter. After
   butter melts, add garlic, chilli and
   breadcrumbs; cook, stirring, until
   breadcrumbs are browned lightly.
3 Combine drained hot pasta and
   breadcrumb mixture in large
   bowl with parsley, lemon rind and
   remaining oil.

serves 4
per serving 30.9g fat;
2916kJ (697 cal)

pumpkin and fetta pies

PREPARATION TIME **10 MINUTES** COOKING TIME **20 MINUTES**

500g pumpkin, cut into
  2cm pieces
3 eggs, beaten lightly
200g fetta, cut into 2cm pieces
2 tablespoons finely grated
  parmesan cheese
2 tablespoons sour cream
1/3 cup (80g) drained
  char-grilled capsicum
  in oil, sliced thinly
2 tablespoons halved seeded
  kalamata olives
4 green onions, sliced thinly
1 sheet ready-rolled puff
  pastry, thawed
1 teaspoon finely shredded
  fresh basil

1 Preheat oven to hot. Grease four
  11cm pie dishes.
2 Boil, steam or microwave
  pumpkin until just tender; drain.
3 Meanwhile, combine egg,
  cheeses, sour cream, capsicum,
  olive and onion in large bowl.
  Add pumpkin; toss gently
  to combine.
4 Cut pastry sheet into four
  squares; press each square
  into a prepared dish, allowing
  pastry to hang over edge. Place
  dishes on oven tray, divide filling
  among dishes.
5 Bake pies, uncovered, in hot
  oven about 15 minutes or until
  filling sets. Sprinkle with basil just
  before serving.

serves 4
per serving 33.7g fat;
2024kJ (484 cal)
serving suggestion Serve pies
with a fresh garden salad.

quick-and-easy prawn and pea risotto

PREPARATION TIME **5 MINUTES** COOKING TIME **25 MINUTES**

600g cooked large prawns
20g butter
1 small leek (200g), sliced thinly
2 cloves garlic, crushed
8 saffron threads
2 cups (400g) arborio rice
2 cups (500ml) boiling water
1 cup (250ml) dry white wine
1½ cups (375ml) fish stock
1 cup (160g) frozen peas
2 tablespoons coarsely
   chopped fresh chives
¼ cup (60ml) lemon juice
30g butter, extra

1 Shell and devein prawns, leaving
tails intact.

2 Place butter, leek, garlic and
saffron in large microwave-safe
bowl; cook in microwave oven
on HIGH (100%), covered, about
2 minutes or until leek softens.
Stir in rice; cook on HIGH
(100%), covered, 1 minute. Add
the water, wine and stock; cook
on HIGH (100%), covered,
15 minutes, pausing to stir
3 times during cooking.

3 Add peas and prawns (reserve
a few for garnish, if desired);
cook on HIGH (100%), covered,
3 minutes. Stir in chives, juice
and extra butter.

serves 4
per serving 12.2g fat; 2574kJ (615 cal)
tip Fresh peas are lovely but of course take extra time to shell and cook. If you
wish to substitute them for frozen, you need about 500g of fresh unshelled
peas for this recipe.

roasted pear, witlof and spinach salad

PREPARATION TIME **10 MINUTES**   COOKING TIME **25 MINUTES**

6 corella pears (600g)
2 teaspoons sugar
6 fresh medium figs (360g)
6 white witlof (750g)
200g baby spinach leaves
2/3 cup (70g) toasted walnuts,
   chopped coarsely
1 tablespoon white wine vinegar
1/4 cup (60ml) orange juice
1/2 cup (125ml) olive oil
1 clove garlic, crushed
100g gorgonzola cheese,
   chopped finely

1 Preheat oven to moderate.
2 Quarter and core pears; place
   in large lightly oiled deep baking
   dish. Sprinkle pear with sugar;
   bake, uncovered, in moderate
   oven about 25 minutes or until
   tender, turning halfway through
   baking time.
3 Meanwhile, cut figs into wedges.
   Separate witlof leaves. Place fig
   and witlof in large serving bowl
   with spinach and walnuts.
4 Combine vinegar, juice, oil and
   garlic in screw-top jar; shake
   well. Add pear, cheese and
   dressing to salad; toss gently
   to combine. Serve with a loaf of
   crusty French bread, if desired.

serves 4
per serving 49.5g fat; 2570kJ (614 cal)
tips Witlof, also known as witloof, Belgian endive or chicory, has crunchy,
slightly bitter leaves; substitute radicchio if desired.
If corella pears are unavailable, use small packham or beurre bosc pears.
Pears can be roasted a day ahead; cover and refrigerate overnight. Dressing
can be made a day ahead but it is best not to assemble this salad until just
before serving.

grilled chicken with herbed butter, almonds and gruyère

PREPARATION TIME **15 MINUTES** COOKING TIME **20 MINUTES**

80g butter, softened
1 tablespoon finely chopped
    fresh flat-leaf parsley
2 teaspoons lemon juice
4 single chicken breast
    fillets (680g)
3 medium carrots (360g), cut
    into thin 8cm matchsticks
250g baby green beans
1/4 cup (35g) toasted
    slivered almonds
1/4 cup (30g) finely grated
    gruyère cheese

1 Combine butter, parsley
   and juice in small bowl,
   cover; refrigerate.
2 Cook chicken on heated oiled
   grill plate (or grill or barbecue)
   until browned both sides and
   cooked through. Cover loosely
   to keep warm.
3 Meanwhile, boil, steam or
   microwave carrot and beans,
   separately, until tender; drain.
4 Serve chicken on vegetables;
   divide parsley butter among
   chicken pieces, sprinkle with
   nuts and cheese.

serves 4
per serving 33.1g fat;
2061kJ (492 cal)

parmesan-breaded lamb cutlets

PREPARATION TIME **15 MINUTES**   COOKING TIME **15 MINUTES**

1/3 cup (50g) plain flour
12 lamb cutlets (900g)
2 eggs
2 tablespoons milk
1 clove garlic, crushed
1/2 cup (35g) stale breadcrumbs
1/2 cup (50g) packaged
   breadcrumbs
1/2 cup (40g) finely grated
   parmesan cheese
1 tablespoon finely chopped
   fresh oregano
2 tablespoons olive oil

1 Place flour in plastic bag. Add
   cutlets; toss to coat cutlets all
   over, shake off excess flour.
2 Combine eggs, milk and garlic in
   medium shallow bowl; combine
   breadcrumbs, cheese and
   oregano in another medium
   shallow bowl. Dip cutlets, one at
   a time, into egg mixture, then in
   breadcrumb mixture.
3 Heat oil in large non-stick frying
   pan; cook cutlets, in batches,
   until browned both sides and
   cooked as desired. Sprinkle
   with fresh whole oregano leaves,
   if desired.

serves 4
per serving 25.1g fat;
1903kJ (455 cal)
serving suggestion Serve with
fetta and black olive mash (p77).

lamb with white wine and mascarpone sauce

PREPARATION TIME 10 MINUTES COOKING TIME 15 MINUTES

¼ cup (60ml) olive oil
12 fresh sage leaves
100g sliced prosciutto
8 lamb steaks (640g)
1 clove garlic, crushed
¾ cup (180ml) dry white wine
½ cup (120g) mascarpone
¼ cup (60ml) cream

1 Heat oil in medium frying pan; cook sage until crisp. Drain on absorbent paper. Cook prosciutto, stirring, until crisp; drain on absorbent paper.
2 Cook lamb in same pan until browned both sides and cooked as desired. Remove from pan.
3 Cook garlic in same pan, stirring, until fragrant. Add wine; bring to a boil. Reduce heat; simmer, uncovered, until liquid reduces by half. Add mascarpone and cream; cook, stirring, over heat until sauce boils and thickens slightly.
4 Divide lamb among serving plates; top with prosciutto and sage, drizzle with sauce.

serves 4
per serving 49.9g fat;
2650kJ (633 cal)
serving suggestion Serve with steamed asparagus.

salmon with peas and green onion

PREPARATION TIME **15 MINUTES** COOKING TIME **15 MINUTES**

60g butter
4 salmon fillets (800g)
2 cloves garlic, crushed
2 medium brown onions (300g),
  sliced thinly
3/4 cup (180ml) fish stock
2 tablespoons lemon juice
1 1/2 cups (185g) frozen peas
8 green onions, trimmed, cut
  into 4cm pieces
1 tablespoon finely grated
  lemon rind
1 teaspoon sea salt flakes

1 Melt half of the butter in large
   heated frying pan; cook salmon
   until browned both sides. Remove
   from pan; cover to keep warm.
2 Melt remaining butter in same
   pan; cook garlic and brown
   onion, stirring, until onion
   softens. Add stock, juice, peas
   and green onion; bring to a
   boil. Reduce heat; simmer,
   uncovered, 2 minutes.
3 Return salmon to pan; sprinkle
   with rind and salt. Cook,
   uncovered, until salmon is
   cooked as desired.

serves 4
per serving 27g fat;
1920kJ (459 cal)

ricotta gnocchi in fresh tomato sauce

PREPARATION TIME **10 MINUTES** COOKING TIME **20 MINUTES**

The Italian word for dumplings, gnocchi can be based on potato, flour, ricotta or polenta. Eggs and parmesan are usually added to the dough, which is then formed into little balls or shell shapes, cooked briefly in boiling water and served topped with butter, more parmesan or one of a myriad savoury sauces.

500g firm ricotta cheese
1 cup (80g) finely grated parmesan cheese
1/2 cup (75g) plain flour
2 eggs, beaten lightly
1 tablespoon extra virgin olive oil
4 medium tomatoes (760g), chopped coarsely
6 green onions, sliced thinly
2 tablespoons coarsely chopped fresh oregano
2 tablespoons balsamic vinegar
2 tablespoons extra virgin olive oil, extra
1/2 cup (40g) shaved parmesan cheese

1 Bring large saucepan of water to a boil.
2 Meanwhile, combine ricotta, grated parmesan, flour, eggs and oil in large bowl. Drop rounded tablespoons of mixture into boiling water; cook, without stirring, until gnocchi float to the surface. Remove from pan with slotted spoon; drain, cover to keep warm.
3 Combine tomato, onion, oregano and vinegar in medium bowl. Top warm gnocchi with fresh tomato sauce; drizzle with extra oil, top with shaved parmesan.

serves 4
per serving 40.6g fat; 2387kJ (570 cal)

grilled octopus salad

PREPARATION TIME **15 MINUTES**   COOKING TIME **5 MINUTES**

⅓ cup (80ml) orange juice

1 tablespoon lemon juice

⅔ cup (160ml) olive oil

1 clove garlic, crushed

600g cleaned baby octopus

1 cup (150g) seeded
    kalamata olives

5 lebanese cucumbers (650g),
    seeded, chopped coarsely

200g grape tomatoes, halved

⅓ cup coarsely chopped fresh
    flat-leaf parsley

1 Combine juices, oil and garlic in
   screw-top jar; shake well.

2 Cook octopus, in batches, on
   heated oiled grill plate (or grill or
   barbecue) until browned lightly
   and cooked as desired. Toss
   octopus and dressing in medium
   bowl; add olives, cucumber,
   tomato and parsley. Toss gently
   to combine.

serves 4
per serving 39.6g fat;
2368kJ (566 cal)

tip Grape tomatoes are a
newcomer to the tomato tray
and are so delicious they're
worth seeking out. However, if
you can't find them, substitute
cherry tomatoes.

grilled scallops with pawpaw salsa

PREPARATION TIME 15 MINUTES   COOKING TIME 10 MINUTES

800g firm pawpaw,
 chopped coarsely
2 medium tomatoes (380g),
 seeded, chopped coarsely
1 medium red onion (170g),
 chopped coarsely
¼ cup (60ml) lime juice
1 red thai chilli, seeded,
 chopped finely
2 tablespoons coarsely
 chopped fresh coriander
1 tablespoon vegetable oil
36 scallops with roe

1 Combine pawpaw, tomato,
 onion, juice, chilli, coriander and
 oil in large bowl.
2 Cook scallops on heated oiled
 grill plate, in batches, until
 browned both sides.
3 Serve pawpaw salsa topped
 with scallops, accompanied by
 sweet chilli sauce, if desired.

serves 4
per serving 5.7g fat;
809kJ (193 cal)

char-grilled tuna salad

PREPARATION TIME **10 MINUTES** COOKING TIME **5 MINUTES**

600g tuna steak
¹/₄ cup (60ml) mirin
1 tablespoon light soy sauce
1 clove garlic, crushed
1 red thai chilli, seeded,
  chopped finely
1 green onion, chopped finely
2 medium red capsicums
  (400g), sliced thinly
200g mesclun

1 Cook tuna on heated oiled
  grill plate (or grill or barbecue)
  until browned both sides and
  cooked as desired. Cover, rest
  2 minutes; cut into thick slices.
2 Meanwhile, combine mirin, soy
  sauce, garlic, chilli and onion in
  screw-top jar; shake well.
3 Combine tuna and dressing in
  large bowl with capsicum and
  mesclun; toss gently to combine.

serves 4
per serving 8.9g fat;
1153kJ (275 cal)
tip Brushing the whole piece of
tuna with olive oil 3 hours ahead
of cooking will help keep it moist
and soft when it's grilled.

prawn, endive and pink grapefruit with lime aïoli

PREPARATION TIME **30 MINUTES**

3 small pink grapefruits (1kg)
1kg cooked large prawns
350g curly endive, torn
1/4 cup coarsely chopped chives
2 trimmed celery sticks (150g),
   sliced thinly
1 small red onion (100g),
   sliced thinly
LIME AIOLI
2 egg yolks
2 teaspoons dijon mustard
1/2 teaspoon finely grated
   lime rind
2 tablespoons lime juice
2 cloves garlic, quartered
3/4 cup (180ml) light olive oil
1 tablespoon hot water

1 Peel grapefruits; separate the
   segments. Shell and devein
   prawns, leaving tails intact.
2 Combine grapefruit and prawns
   in large serving bowl with
   remaining ingredients. Serve
   with lime aïoli.
   lime aïoli Blend or process egg
   yolks, mustard, rind, juice and
   garlic until combined. With motor
   operating, gradually add oil,
   blending until aïoli thickens. With
   motor operating, add enough
   of the water (if any) to achieve
   desired consistency.

serves 4
per serving 45.6g fat;
2297kJ (549 cal)
tip Lime aïoli can be prepared
a day ahead; keep, covered,
under refrigeration.

steak diane

PREPARATION TIME 10 MINUTES   COOKING TIME 15 MINUTES

1 tablespoon olive oil

8 thin slices beef fillet (800g)

20g butter

3 cloves garlic, crushed

3 green onions, sliced thinly

1 tablespoon brandy

2 tablespoons worcestershire
   sauce

300ml cream

1 Heat oil in large frying pan; cook
   beef, in batches, until browned
   both sides and cooked as
   desired. Cover to keep warm.

2 Melt butter in same pan; cook
   garlic and onion, stirring, until
   onion softens. Add brandy and
   sauce; bring to a boil. Stir in
   cream, reduce heat; simmer,
   uncovered, about 3 minutes or
   until sauces thickens slightly.

3 Divide beef equally among
   serving plates; top with sauce.

serves 4
per serving 51.1g fat;
2755kJ (658 cal)
serving suggestion Serve steak
diane with french fries.

crisp beef with baby bok choy and noodles

PREPARATION TIME 15 MINUTES COOKING TIME 15 MINUTES

2 tablespoons cornflour
1/2 teaspoon bicarbonate
 of soda
600g beef rump steak,
 cut into thin strips
2/3 cup (160ml) peanut oil
2 tablespoons sweet
 chilli sauce
1/4 cup (60ml) keçap manis
1 tablespoon light soy sauce
2 teaspoons sesame oil
1 clove garlic, crushed
2 green onions, chopped finely
400g fresh thin egg noodles
200g shiitake mushrooms,
 quartered
1/2 small chinese cabbage
 (400g), shredded coarsely
300g baby bok choy, sliced
 thinly lengthways

1 Combine cornflour and soda in
 large bowl. Add beef; toss to
 coat all over, shaking off excess.
2 Heat a third of the peanut oil in
 wok or large frying pan; stir-fry
 about a third of the beef until
 crisp. Drain on absorbent paper,
 then cover to keep warm; repeat
 with remaining peanut oil and beef.
3 Combine sauces, sesame oil,
 garlic and onion in small bowl.
4 Place noodles in large heatproof
 bowl, cover with boiling water;
 separate with fork, drain.
5 Reheat same cleaned wok;
 stir-fry mushrooms about
 2 minutes or until just tender.
 Add cabbage and bok choy;
 stir-fry 1 minute. Add sauce
 mixture, noodles and beef;
 stir-fry until heated through.

serves 4
per serving 47.3g fat; 3605kJ (861 cal)
tip You can buy beef strips instead of a piece of
rump to save time.

fettuccine boscaiola with chicken

PREPARATION TIME **10 MINUTES** COOKING TIME **10 MINUTES**

The pasta sauce known as boscaiola translates roughly as woodcutter's sauce, a name thought to have evolved from the fact that Italian woodsmen made good use of the fungi harvested from beneath the trees they felled, back at their campfire at night. You need about half a large barbecued chicken for this recipe.

500g fettuccine
1 tablespoon olive oil
1 medium brown onion (150g), chopped finely
2 bacon rashers (140g), chopped finely
200g button mushrooms, sliced finely
$1/4$ cup (60ml) dry white wine
$2/3$ cup (160ml) cream
1 cup (250ml) milk
1 cup (170g) thinly sliced cooked chicken
$1/4$ cup (20g) finely grated parmesan cheese
2 tablespoons coarsely chopped fresh flat-leaf parsley

1 Cook pasta in large saucepan of boiling water, uncovered, until just tender; drain, reserving $1/2$ cup of cooking liquid.
2 Meanwhile, heat oil in large saucepan; cook onion, stirring, until soft. Add bacon and mushrooms; cook, stirring, 1 minute.
3 Add wine, cream and milk; bring to a boil. Reduce heat; simmer, stirring, 5 minutes. Add chicken; stir until combined.
4 Add pasta, cheese, parsley and reserved cooking liquid; toss gently over low heat until hot.

serves 4
per serving 32.9g fat; 3425kJ (818 cal)
tip Fresh basil can be used instead of parsley, if you prefer.

prawn, lime and rice noodle stir-fry

PREPARATION TIME **20 MINUTES** COOKING TIME **10 MINUTES**

650g uncooked large prawns
375g thick rice stick noodles
1 tablespoon sesame oil
2 cloves garlic, crushed
2 teaspoons grated fresh ginger
2 red thai chillies, seeded,
  sliced thinly
250g broccolini, quartered
1/3 cup (80ml) lime juice
1/4 cup (60ml) light soy sauce
2 teaspoons fish sauce
4 green onions, sliced thinly
2 tablespoons coarsely
  chopped fresh mint

1 Shell and devein prawns, leaving
   tails intact.
2 Place noodles in large heatproof
   bowl, cover with boiling water;
   stand until just tender, drain.
3 Meanwhile, heat oil in wok or
   large frying pan; stir-fry garlic,
   ginger and chilli until fragrant.
   Add broccolini; stir-fry until just
   tender. Add prawns; stir-fry
   until just changed in colour.
   Add noodles and remaining
   ingredients; stir-fry until hot.

serves 4
per serving 6.5g fat;
1769kJ (423 cal)
tip Broccolini, sweeter than
broccoli with a subtle peppery
edge, is completely edible, from
flower to stem. Substitute gai
larn or broccoli if broccolini is
not available.

veal with mushrooms and mustard cream sauce

PREPARATION TIME **5 MINUTES**   COOKING TIME **20 MINUTES**

1 tablespoon olive oil
8 veal steaks (640g)
10g butter
1 clove garlic, crushed
150g button mushrooms,
  sliced thickly
1/3 cup (80ml) dry white wine
1 tablespoon wholegrain
  mustard
1/2 cup (125ml) cream
1/4 cup (60ml) chicken stock
1 teaspoon fresh thyme leaves

1 Heat oil in large non-stick frying
   pan; cook veal, in batches, until
   browned both sides and cooked
   as desired. Cover to keep warm.
2 Melt butter in same pan; cook
   garlic and mushrooms, stirring,
   until mushrooms just soften. Add
   wine and mustard; cook, stirring,
   2 minutes. Add cream and
   stock; bring to a boil. Reduce
   heat; simmer, uncovered, about
   5 minutes or until sauce thickens
   slightly. Stir in thyme.
3 Divide veal equally among
   serving plates; top with sauce.

serves 4
per serving 24.4g fat;
1612kJ (385 cal)
serving suggestion Serve veal
with farfalle (bow-tie pasta).

fish fillets pan-fried with pancetta and caper herb butter

PREPARATION TIME **15 MINUTES**   COOKING TIME **10 MINUTES**

We used snapper fillets for this recipe, but any firm white fish fillet can be used.

80g butter, softened
2 tablespoons coarsely chopped fresh flat-leaf parsley
1 tablespoon capers, rinsed, drained
2 cloves garlic, quartered
2 green onions, chopped coarsely
8 slices pancetta (120g)
4 white fish fillets (600g)
1 tablespoon olive oil
350g asparagus, trimmed

1 Blend or process butter, parsley, capers, garlic and onion until mixture forms a smooth paste.

2 Spread 1 heaped tablespoon of the butter mixture and two slices of the pancetta on each fish fillet.

3 Heat oil in large heavy-base frying pan; cook fish, pancetta-butter side down, until pancetta is crisp. Turn fish carefully; cook, uncovered, until cooked as desired.

4 Meanwhile, boil, steam or microwave asparagus until tender.

5 Serve fish and asparagus drizzled with pan juices.

serves 4
per serving 28.5g fat; 1731kJ (414 cal)

red beef curry

PREPARATION TIME **10 MINUTES** COOKING TIME **20 MINUTES**

2 tablespoons peanut oil
500g beef rump, cut into
    2cm pieces
1 large brown onion (200g),
    sliced thinly
1/4 cup (75g) red curry paste
1 large red capsicum (350g),
    sliced thinly
150g snake beans, chopped
1²/₃ cups (400ml) coconut milk
425g can crushed tomatoes
1/4 cup coarsely chopped
    fresh coriander

1 Heat half of the oil in wok or
   large frying pan; stir-fry beef, in
   batches, until browned all over.
2 Heat remaining oil in same wok;
   stir-fry onion until soft. Add
   paste; stir-fry until fragrant. Add
   capsicum and snake beans;
   stir-fry until vegetables just soften.
3 Return beef to wok with remaining
   ingredients; stir-fry until sauce
   thickens slightly.

serves 4
per serving 41.9g fat;
2390kJ (571 cal)
serving suggestion Serve with
steamed jasmine rice.

hokkien noodle and pork stir-fry

PREPARATION TIME 20 MINUTES COOKING TIME **10 MINUTES**

600g hokkien noodles
1 tablespoon cornflour
1/2 cup (125ml) water
1/4 cup (60ml) keçap manis
1/4 cup (60ml) hoisin sauce
2 tablespoons rice vinegar
2 tablespoons peanut oil
600g pork fillet, sliced thinly
1 medium brown onion (150g),
 sliced thickly
2 cloves garlic, crushed
1 teaspoon grated fresh ginger
150g sugar snap peas, trimmed
1 medium red capsicum (200g),
 sliced thinly
1 medium yellow capsicum
 (200g), sliced thinly
200g baby bok choy, quartered

1 Place noodles in large heatproof
 bowl, cover with boiling water.
 Separate noodles with fork; drain.
2 Blend cornflour with the water
 in small bowl; stir in sauces
 and vinegar.
3 Heat half of the oil in wok or
 large frying pan; stir-fry pork, in
 batches, until browned all over.
4 Heat remaining oil in wok;
 stir-fry onion, garlic and ginger
 until onion softens. Add peas,
 capsicums and bok choy; stir-fry
 until vegetables are just tender.
5 Return pork to wok with noodles
 and sauce mixture; stir-fry until
 sauce thickens slightly.

serves 4
per serving 14.3g fat;
2180kJ (521 cal)

baked mustard pork with caramelised apple

PREPARATION TIME **10 MINUTES** COOKING TIME **25 MINUTES**

1 medium red onion (170g),
  cut into thin wedges
1 tablespoon olive oil
750g pork fillets, trimmed
1/2 cup (140g) honey dijon
  wholegrain mustard
1/2 cup (125ml) apple juice
1/3 cup (80ml) vegetable stock
1/4 cup coarsely chopped fresh
  flat-leaf parsley
60g butter
4 large apples (800g), peeled,
  cored, sliced thinly
2 tablespoons brown sugar

1 Preheat oven to very hot.
2 Combine onion and oil in large
   flameproof baking dish. Brush
   pork all over with mustard; place
   on onion in baking dish. Bake,
   uncovered, in very hot oven
   about 20 minutes or until cooked
   as desired. Remove pork from
   dish, cover; rest 5 minutes.
3 Place dish over heat; add
   juice and stock, bring to a
   boil. Reduce heat; simmer,
   uncovered, about 3 minutes
   or until sauce thickens slightly.
   Stir in parsley.
4 Meanwhile, melt butter in large
   frying pan. Add apple and sugar;
   cook, stirring occasionally,
   about 10 minutes or until
   almost caramelised. Cover
   to keep warm.
5 Slice pork thickly; serve with
   onion sauce and apple.

serves 4
per serving 22.5g fat;
2110kJ (504 cal)
serving suggestion Accompany
with a watercress salad, if desired.

roasted mediterranean-style fish and vegetables

PREPARATION TIME 5 MINUTES   COOKING TIME 25 MINUTES

2 x 425g cans whole new
   potatoes, rinsed, drained
250g cherry tomatoes
1 whole garlic bulb, separated
   into unpeeled cloves
2 large red onions (600g),
   chopped coarsely
3 rosemary sprigs,
   chopped coarsely
1/4 cup (60ml) olive oil
8 x 75g skinless bream fillets
1/4 cup (60ml) lemon juice
1/4 cup firmly packed fresh
   basil leaves

1 Preheat oven to hot.
2 Place potatoes and tomatoes
   in large lightly oiled baking dish;
   crush slightly with potato masher.
   Sprinkle garlic, onion and
   rosemary into baking dish;
   drizzle with half of the oil.
3 Roast vegetables, uncovered, in
   hot oven for 15 minutes. Place
   fish on vegetables, sprinkle with
   juice and remaining oil; bake,
   uncovered, in hot oven about
   10 minutes or until fish is
   cooked as desired. Sprinkle
   with basil leaves.

serves 4
per serving 22.1g fat;
1931kJ (461 cal)

spicy roasted pumpkin couscous

PREPARATION TIME 10 MINUTES COOKING TIME 20 MINUTES

1 tablespoon olive oil
2 cloves garlic, crushed
1 large red onion (200g),
  sliced thickly
500g pumpkin, peeled,
  chopped coarsely
3 teaspoons ground cumin
2 teaspoons ground coriander
1 cup (200g) couscous
1 cup (250ml) boiling water
20g butter
2 tablespoons coarsely chopped
  fresh flat-leaf parsley

1 Preheat oven to hot.
2 Heat oil in medium flameproof
   baking dish; cook garlic, onion
   and pumpkin, stirring, until
   vegetables are browned lightly.
   Add spices; cook, stirring, about
   2 minutes or until fragrant.
3 Place baking dish in hot
   oven; roast pumpkin mixture,
   uncovered, about 15 minutes or
   until pumpkin is just tender.
4 Meanwhile, combine couscous
   with the water and butter in
   large heatproof bowl; cover,
   stand about 5 minutes or until
   water is absorbed, fluffing with
   fork occasionally.
5 Add pumpkin mixture to
   couscous; stir in parsley.

serves 4
per serving 9.8g fat;
1361kJ (325 cal)

lamb's lettuce, avocado and tomato salad

PREPARATION TIME **15 MINUTES**

Lamb's lettuce, also known as mâche or corn salad, has a mild, almost
nutty flavour and tender, narrow, dark-green leaves.

60g lamb's lettuce
250g yellow teardrop
    tomatoes, halved
250g cherry tomatoes, halved
1 small red onion (100g),
    sliced thinly
1 medium avocado (250g),
    chopped coarsely
¼ cup coarsely chopped fresh
    flat-leaf parsley
1 tablespoon finely shredded
    fresh basil
¼ cup (60ml) extra virgin
    olive oil
2 tablespoons balsamic vinegar
1 teaspoon brown sugar
1 clove garlic, crushed

1 Combine lamb's lettuce,
   tomatoes, onion, avocado and
   herbs in large serving bowl.
2 Combine remaining ingredients in
   screw-top jar; shake well.
3 Pour dressing over salad; toss
   gently to combine.

serves 4
per serving 23.8g fat;
1020kJ (244 cal)

sumac wedges

PREPARATION TIME 5 MINUTES COOKING TIME 25 MINUTES

Sumac, a granular spice ranging in colour from a deep terracotta to almost-black purple, is used extensively from the eastern Mediterranean through to Pakistan. Both in cooking and as a condiment, sumac's tart astringency adds a delightful piquancy to food without the heat of a chilli.

1kg sebago potatoes, washed
2 tablespoons sumac
2 tablespoons olive oil

1 Preheat oven to very hot. Lightly grease oven tray.
2 Cut potatoes into wedges; combine in large microwave-safe bowl with sumac and oil.
3 Cook, covered, in microwave oven, on HIGH (100%), for 5 minutes.
4 Place wedges, in single layer, on prepared tray. Roast, uncovered, in very hot oven about 20 minutes or until wedges are crisp. Sprinkle with sea salt flakes, if desired.

serves 4
per serving 9.8g fat;
956kJ (228 cal)

baby beet salad

PREPARATION TIME 20 MINUTES

850g can whole baby beets,
    rinsed, drained, quartered
1 cup (80g) bean sprouts
1 medium carrot (120g),
    sliced thinly
1 trimmed celery stick (75g),
    sliced thinly
1 small red onion (100g),
    sliced thinly
1/2 cup loosely packed fresh
    mint leaves
1 tablespoon finely grated
    lime rind
1/4 cup (60ml) lime juice
2 tablespoons olive oil

1 Place beets, sprouts, carrot,
    celery, onion and mint in large
    serving bowl.
2 Combine remaining ingredients in
    screw-top jar; shake well.
3 Drizzle dressing over salad; toss
    gently to combine.

serves 4
per serving 9.4g fat;
707kJ (169 cal)

chats with black mustard seeds and sea salt

PREPARATION TIME **5 MINUTES** COOKING TIME **25 MINUTES**

Tiny, waxy immature potatoes, harvested early in the season, are known as chats, baby potatoes or new potatoes.

1kg tiny new potatoes
2 tablespoons olive oil
1 tablespoon black
   mustard seeds
2 teaspoons sea salt flakes
1 teaspoon freshly ground
   black pepper
1 tablespoon coarsely chopped
   fresh flat-leaf parsley

1 Boil, steam or microwave
   potatoes until just tender; drain.
2 Heat oil in large frying pan; cook
   potatoes, stirring, until potatoes
   are browned lightly. Add mustard
   seeds, stirring, about 1 minute or
   until seeds pop.
3 Add remaining ingredients; toss
   gently to combine.

serves 4
per serving 9.5g fat;
1033kJ (247 cal)

snow pea stir-fry with sesame seeds and pine nuts

PREPARATION TIME **10 MINUTES** COOKING TIME **10 MINUTES**

1 tablespoon sesame oil
600g snow peas, trimmed
2 green onions, sliced thinly
2 tablespoons toasted
   pine nuts
1 tablespoon toasted
   sesame seeds

1 Heat oil in wok or large frying
   pan; stir-fry snow peas and
   onion about 5 minutes or until
   snow peas are just tender.
2 Add nuts and seeds to wok;
   stir-fry briefly to combine.

serves 4
per serving 11.5g fat;
657kJ (157 cal)

white bean salad with coriander, mint and lemon grass

PREPARATION TIME **15 MINUTES**

2 x 400g cans cannellini beans, rinsed, drained
150g baby spinach leaves
1 small red onion (100g), sliced thinly
1 clove garlic, crushed
1 tablespoon coarsely chopped fresh coriander
1 tablespoon coarsely chopped fresh mint
1 tablespoon thinly sliced fresh lemon grass
1 teaspoon grated fresh ginger
2 tablespoons sesame oil
2 tablespoons soy sauce
2 tablespoons sweet chilli sauce
2 tablespoons lime juice
1 teaspoon honey
2 red thai chillies, seeded, sliced thinly

1 Combine beans in large bowl with spinach and onion.
2 Combine garlic, herbs, lemon grass, ginger, oil, sauces, juice and honey in screw-top jar; shake well.
3 Just before serving, drizzle dressing over salad; toss gently to combine, then sprinkle with chilli.

serves 4
per serving 9.8g fat; 558kJ (133 cal)

spiced lentils

PREPARATION TIME **5 MINUTES** COOKING TIME **15 MINUTES**

1½ cups (300g) red lentils
50g butter
1 small brown onion (80g),
  chopped finely
1 clove garlic, crushed
½ teaspoon ground coriander
½ teaspoon ground cumin
¼ teaspoon ground turmeric
¼ teaspoon cayenne pepper
½ cup (125ml) chicken stock
2 tablespoons coarsely
  chopped fresh
  flat-leaf parsley

1 Cook lentils, uncovered, in large
  saucepan of boiling water until
  just tender; drain.
2 Meanwhile, melt half of the butter
  in large frying pan; cook onion,
  garlic and spices, stirring, until
  onion softens.
3 Add lentils, stock and remaining
  butter; cook, stirring, until hot.
  Stir parsley into lentils off the heat.

serves 4
per serving 12.1g fat;
1248kJ (298 cal)

brussels sprouts and sun-dried tomato stir-fry

PREPARATION TIME **15 MINUTES**   COOKING TIME **10 MINUTES**

1kg brussels sprouts
2 tablespoons olive oil
1 clove garlic, crushed
1/4 cup (35g) drained sun-dried
   tomatoes, sliced thinly
1/4 cup (40g) toasted pine nuts
2 tablespoons lemon juice

1 Trim sprouts; slice thickly.
2 Heat half of the oil in wok or
   large frying pan; stir-fry sprouts
   and garlic until sprouts are
   just tender.
3 Add tomato, nuts, juice and
   remaining oil; toss gently until
   heated through.

serves 4
per serving 17.6g fat;
1028kJ (246 cal)

greek salad with taramasalata dressing

PREPARATION TIME **20 MINUTES**

Greek taramasalata is a robust but creamy dip made with smoked fish (usually cod or carp) roe, lemon juice, breadcrumbs, olive oil and various seasonings. It's readily available from the deli section at your local supermarket.

1 small red onion (100g)
2 medium egg tomatoes
    (300g), quartered
2 lebanese cucumbers (260g),
    sliced thickly
1 medium green capsicum
    (200g), sliced thickly
1 small cos lettuce, torn
½ cup (80g) seeded
    kalamata olives
150g fetta cheese,
    chopped coarsely
1 tablespoon coarsely chopped
    fresh oregano
1 tablespoon coarsely chopped
    fresh flat-leaf parsley
1 tablespoon lemon juice
2 tablespoons olive oil
⅓ cup (90g) taramasalata

1 Cut onion into thin wedges.
2 Combine onion in large bowl with
    tomato, cucumber, capsicum,
    lettuce, olives and cheese.
3 Sprinkle herbs over salad then
    drizzle with combined remaining
    ingredients; serve without tossing.

serves 4
per serving 22.9g fat;
1279kJ (306 cal)
serving suggestion This salad
is ideal with barbecued octopus
or lamb.

cheesy pesto polenta

PREPARATION TIME **10 MINUTES**   COOKING TIME **25 MINUTES**

2$\frac{1}{3}$ cups (580ml) water
2$\frac{1}{3}$ cups (580ml) milk
1 cup (170g) polenta
$\frac{1}{2}$ cup (40g) finely grated
   parmesan cheese
30g butter, chopped
PESTO
2 tablespoons finely grated
   parmesan cheese
2 tablespoons toasted
   pine nuts
2 tablespoons olive oil
1 clove garlic, crushed
1 cup firmly packed fresh
   basil leaves

1 Combine the water and milk in
large saucepan; bring to a boil.
Gradually sprinkle polenta over
milk mixture; cook, stirring, until
polenta thickens slightly.
2 Reduce heat; simmer,
uncovered, about 20 minutes
or until polenta is thickened,
stirring occasionally. Stir in
cheese, butter and pesto.
pesto Blend or process
ingredients until mixture
forms a paste.

serves 4
per serving 31.3g fat;
2023kJ (483 cal)

fresh corn and zucchini chunky salsa

PREPARATION TIME I0 MINUTES COOKING TIME **I0 MINUTES**

2 corn cobs (800g), trimmed
100g baby zucchini,
    halved lengthways
2 large avocados (640g),
    chopped coarsely
200g grape tomatoes, halved
1 medium red onion (170g),
    halved, sliced thickly
1/4 cup coarsely chopped
    fresh coriander
1 tablespoon sweet chilli sauce
1/3 cup (80ml) lime juice
2 red thai chillies, seeded,
    sliced thinly

1 Cook corn and zucchini on
   heated oiled grill plate (or grill or
   barbecue) until browned lightly
   and tender. Using a sharp knife,
   remove corn kernels from cobs.
2 Combine corn and zucchini in
   large serving bowl with avocado,
   tomato, onion and coriander.
3 Place remaining ingredients in
   screw-top jar; shake well. Drizzle
   dressing over salsa; toss gently
   to combine.

serves 4
per serving 27.4g fat;
1704kJ (407 cal)
tip You can substitute cherry
tomatoes if you cannot obtain
the grape variety.

sweet chilli and lime mixed vegetable salad

PREPARATION TIME **20 MINUTES**   COOKING TIME **5 MINUTES**

200g asparagus, trimmed,
  chopped coarsely
100g fresh baby corn,
  sliced lengthways
1 medium red capsicum (200g),
  sliced thinly
100g shiitake mushrooms,
  sliced thinly
1 lebanese cucumber (130g),
  seeded, sliced thinly
12 green onions, sliced thinly
100g bean sprouts
1 red thai chilli, sliced thinly
2 tablespoons finely chopped
  fresh coriander
2 tablespoons lime juice
1 tablespoon sweet chilli sauce
2 teaspoons sesame oil
2 teaspoons fish sauce
1 clove garlic, crushed

1 Boil, steam or microwave
   asparagus and corn, separately,
   until just tender; drain. Cool.
2 Combine asparagus and
   corn in large serving bowl
   with capsicum, mushrooms,
   cucumber, onion, sprouts,
   chilli and coriander.
3 Place remaining ingredients in
   screw-top jar; shake well. Drizzle
   salad with dressing; toss gently
   to combine.

serves 4
per serving 3.1g fat;
281kJ (91 cal)

caramelised apple tart

PREPARATION TIME **10 MINUTES**   COOKING TIME **20 MINUTES**

4 small apples (520g)
50g butter
¼ cup (55g) firmly packed brown sugar
½ teaspoon ground cinnamon
½ cup (50g) pecans
¼ cup (75g) apple sauce
2 teaspoons lemon juice
2 sheets ready-rolled butter puff pastry
1 egg, beaten lightly

1 Peel and core apples; slice thinly. Stir butter, sugar and cinnamon in medium saucepan over low heat until sugar dissolves; add apple. Cook, stirring occasionally, over low heat, until apple softens. Drain apple mixture over medium bowl; reserve caramel mixture.

2 Meanwhile, blend or process pecans, apple sauce and juice until smooth.

3 Preheat oven to moderately hot. Line oven tray with baking paper.

4 Cut eight 11cm rounds from pastry sheets; place four of the rounds on prepared tray; brush with egg. Using 9cm cutter, remove centres from four remaining rounds; centre pastry rings on top of the 11cm rounds.

5 Spread pecan mixture in centre of rounds; top with apple mixture. Bake tarts, uncovered, in moderately hot oven about 15 minutes or until golden brown. Serve warm, with heated reserved caramel mixture.

serves 4
per serving 39.7g fat; 2606kJ (623 cal)
tip We used granny smith apples in this recipe because their firm white flesh retains its shape and readily absorbs the butter and sugar mixture.

You can use a saucer to cut eight 11cm rounds from the pastry sheets

Any dish can be used to cut away 9cm centres from four of the 11cm rounds

rhubarb galette

PREPARATION TIME **10 MINUTES**   COOKING TIME **20 MINUTES**

You need about four trimmed large stems of rhubarb for this recipe.

20g butter, melted
2½ cups (275g) coarsely
    chopped rhubarb
⅓ cup (75g) firmly packed
    brown sugar
1 teaspoon finely grated
    orange rind
1 sheet ready-rolled puff pastry
2 tablespoons almond meal
10g butter, melted, extra

1 Preheat oven to hot. Line oven tray with baking paper.
2 Combine butter, rhubarb, sugar and rind in medium bowl.
3 Cut 24cm round from pastry, place on prepared tray; sprinkle almond meal evenly over pastry. Spread rhubarb mixture over pastry, leaving a 4cm border. Fold 2cm of pastry edge up and around filling. Brush edge with extra butter.
4 Bake galette, uncovered, in hot oven about 20 minutes or until browned lightly.

serves 4
per serving 18.2g fat;
1326kJ (317 cal)
serving suggestion Serve with scoops of vanilla ice-cream.

tiramisu trifle

PREPARATION TIME **20 MINUTES** (PLUS REFRIGERATION TIME)

1 tablespoon dried
    coffee powder
$1/2$ cup (125ml) boiling water
2 tablespoons sambuca
125g sponge fingers
    (approximately 11 biscuits)
$3/4$ cup (180ml) thickened cream
$1/3$ cup (55g) icing sugar mixture
2 cups (500g) mascarpone
$1/3$ cup (80ml) marsala
2 teaspoons cocoa powder

1 Combine coffee and the water
in small bowl; stir until coffee
dissolves, then stir in liqueur. Cut
biscuits in half crossways.

2 Beat cream, icing sugar and
mascarpone with electric mixer in
small bowl until soft peaks form;
fold in marsala.

3 Dip half of the biscuits in coffee
mixture; divide among four
$1 1/2$-cup (375ml) serving
glasses. Divide half of the
mascarpone mixture among
glasses; dip remaining biscuits
in coffee mixture, divide among
glasses, top with remaining
mascarpone mixture.

4 Dust tiramisu trifles with sifted
cocoa; refrigerate until chilled.

serves 4
per serving 89.8g fat;
4503kJ (1076 cal)
serving suggestion Accompany
trifles with cups of espresso.

red fruit salad with lemon mascarpone

PREPARATION TIME **20 MINUTES**

1kg seedless watermelon
250g strawberries,
    hulled, quartered
150g raspberries
2 medium plums, sliced thinly
1 tablespoon caster sugar
1/3 cup (80ml) kirsch
LEMON MASCARPONE
250g mascarpone
2 teaspoons finely grated
    lemon rind
2 teaspoons caster sugar
1 tablespoon lemon juice

1 Using melon baller, scoop
  watermelon into balls. Place
  watermelon in large serving bowl
  with strawberries, raspberries,
  plums, sugar and liqueur; toss
  gently to combine. Cover;
  refrigerate until ready to serve.
2 Serve fruit salad accompanied
  by lemon mascarpone.
  lemon mascarpone Combine
  ingredients in small bowl.

serves 4
per serving 36.5g fat;
2139kJ (511 cal)

banana caramel puddings

PREPARATION TIME **15 MINUTES** COOKING TIME **15 MINUTES**

90g butter, melted
1/2 cup (60g) almond meal
3 egg whites
3/4 cup (120g) icing
    sugar mixture
1/4 cup (75g) plain flour
50g butter, melted, extra
1/3 cup (75g) firmly packed
    brown sugar
2 medium bananas (400g),
    sliced thickly

1 Preheat oven to moderately hot.
   Grease four deep-sided
   9.5cm ovenproof dishes; place
   on oven tray.
2 Combine butter, almond meal,
   egg whites, icing sugar and flour
   in medium bowl; stir until just
   mixed together.
3 Divide extra butter among
   prepared dishes; sprinkle evenly
   with brown sugar. Divide banana
   slices then pudding mixture
   equally among dishes.
4 Bake, uncovered, in moderately
   hot oven about 15 minutes or
   until puddings are browned
   lightly. Stand puddings 2 minutes;
   turn onto serving plates.

serves 4
per serving 37.3g fat;
2764kJ (660 cal)
serving suggestion Serve with
scoops of vanilla ice-cream.

ice-cream sundae with berry sauce and almond wafers

PREPARATION TIME **20 MINUTES** COOKING TIME **10 MINUTES**

1/3 cup (75g) firmly packed brown sugar
25g butter
1/2 cup (125ml) thickened cream
1 cup (150g) frozen mixed berries
500ml vanilla ice-cream
500ml strawberry ice-cream
ALMOND WAFERS
1 egg white
2 tablespoons caster sugar
2 tablespoons plain flour
20g butter, melted
2 tablespoons flaked almonds

1　Combine sugar, butter and cream in small saucepan; bring to a boil. Reduce heat; simmer, uncovered, stirring, about 5 minutes or until slightly thickened. Remove from heat; stir in berries.

2　Divide both ice-creams among four 1 1/2-cup (375ml) serving glasses; drizzle with berry sauce. Serve with almond wafers.
　　almond wafers Preheat oven to moderate. Lightly grease two oven trays. Beat egg white in small bowl with electric mixer until soft peaks form. Gradually add sugar, beating until dissolved after each addition; fold in flour and butter. Drop rounded teaspoons of mixture 10cm apart on greased oven trays (approximately four per tray); sprinkle with nuts. Bake, uncovered, in moderate oven about 5 minutes or until wafers are browned lightly; cool on trays.

serves 4
per serving 37.2g fat; 2447kJ (585 cal)

nectarines on brioche

PREPARATION TIME 15 MINUTES   COOKING TIME 5 MINUTES

4 nectarines (680g)
40g butter, chopped
1/4 cup (55g) firmly packed
   brown sugar
1/4 teaspoon ground nutmeg
200g mascarpone
1 tablespoon icing
   sugar mixture
1 tablespoon Cointreau
2 teaspoons finely grated
   orange rind
2 small brioche (200g)
2 teaspoons icing sugar
   mixture, extra

1 Halve nectarines; cut each half
   into thirds.
2 Melt butter in medium frying pan;
   add sugar and nutmeg, stir until
   sugar dissolves. Add nectarines;
   cook, stirring, until browned lightly.
3 Meanwhile, combine mascarpone,
   icing sugar, liqueur and rind in
   small bowl. Cut each brioche
   into four slices; toast until
   browned lightly both sides.
4 Divide brioche slices among
   serving plates; top with
   mascarpone mixture and
   nectarine pieces. Dust with extra
   sifted icing sugar.

serves 4
per serving 43g fat;
2679kJ (640 cal)
tip Cointreau is a clear
orange-flavoured brandy.

pear and plum amaretti crumble

PREPARATION TIME **10 MINUTES**   COOKING TIME **15 MINUTES**

825g can plums in syrup,
  drained, halved, stoned
825g can pear halves in natural
  juice, drained, halved
1 teaspoon ground cardamom
125g amaretti (almond
  macaroons), crushed
$1/3$ cup (50g) plain flour
$1/3$ cup (35g) almond meal
$1/2$ cup (70g) slivered almonds
100g butter, chopped

1 Preheat oven to moderately hot.
   Grease deep 6 cup (1.5-litre)
   ovenproof dish.
2 Combine plums, pears and
   cardamom in prepared dish;
   toss gently to combine.
3 Combine amaretti, flour, almond
   meal and nuts in medium bowl.
   Using fingers, rub butter into
   amaretti mixture, sprinkle evenly
   over plum mixture.
4 Bake, uncovered, in moderately
   hot oven about 15 minutes or
   until golden brown.

serves 4
per serving 39.8g fat;
2852kJ (681 cal)
tip Crumbles may also be made
in four 1$1/2$-cup (375ml) individual
dishes and baked for 15 minutes.
serving suggestion Serve with
vanilla custard.

orange and date dessert muffins

PREPARATION TIME **10 MINUTES**   COOKING TIME **20 MINUTES**

2 cups (300g) self-raising flour
1/2 cup (75g) plain flour
1/2 teaspoon bicarbonate
   of soda
1 1/4 cups (250g) firmly packed
   brown sugar
125g butter, melted
1 cup (250ml) buttermilk
1 egg, beaten lightly
2 teaspoons finely grated
   orange rind
1 cup (160g) coarsely chopped
   seeded dates
ORANGE SAUCE
3/4 cup (150g) firmly packed
   brown sugar
2 teaspoons cornflour
1/3 cup (80ml) orange juice
2 tablespoons Grand Marnier
125g butter, chopped
1 tablespoon finely grated
   orange rind

1 Preheat oven to moderately hot.
   Grease and line 12-hole
   (1/3 cup/80ml) muffin pan with
   muffin cases.
2 Sift flours and soda into large
   bowl. Stir in sugar, then add
   butter, buttermilk, egg, rind
   and dates, stirring until just
   combined. Divide mixture
   among muffin cases.
3 Bake muffins, uncovered, in
   moderately hot oven about
   20 minutes. Stand 5 minutes.
   Serve muffins warm with
   orange sauce.
   orange sauce Combine sugar
   and cornflour in small saucepan,
   gradually stir in juice and liqueur;
   bring to a boil, stirring until sauce
   boils and thickens. Stir in butter
   and rind.

makes 12
per muffin 18.4g fat; 1904kJ (455 cal)
tip Grand Marnier is an orange-flavoured liqueur based on cognac brandy.

floating islands in cardamom cream

PREPARATION TIME **15 MINUTES**   COOKING TIME **15 MINUTES**

2 egg whites
1/3 cup (75g) caster sugar
2/3 cup (160ml) cream
2 teaspoons honey
1/2 teaspoon ground cardamom
1/3 cup (60g) coarsely
   chopped pistachios

1   Preheat oven to moderately slow. Grease four 3/4-cup (180ml) ovenproof dishes.

2   Beat egg whites in small bowl with electric mixer until soft peaks form; gradually add sugar, 1 tablespoon at a time, beating until sugar dissolves between additions.

3   Divide egg white mixture among prepared dishes; using spatula, smooth tops. Place dishes in baking dish; pour enough boiling water into large deep baking dish to come halfway up sides of dishes.

4   Bake, uncovered, in moderately slow oven about 12 minutes or until floating islands have risen by about a third. Stand in baking dish 2 minutes.

5   Meanwhile, combine cream, honey and cardamom in small jug.

6   Divide cardamom cream among serving plates; turn floating islands onto cream, sprinkle with nuts.

serves 4
per serving 22.3g fat; 1331kJ (318 cal)
tip   Cardamom cream will intensify in flavour if made a few hours before serving.

105

choc-brownies with caramel sauce

PREPARATION TIME 10 MINUTES   COOKING TIME 20 MINUTES

80g butter

150g dark chocolate, chopped coarsely

$3/4$ cup (150g) firmly packed brown sugar

2 eggs, beaten lightly

1 teaspoon vanilla essence

$3/4$ cup (110g) plain flour

300ml vanilla ice-cream

$1/3$ cup (45g) vienna almonds, chopped coarsely

CARAMEL SAUCE

$2/3$ cup (180ml) cream

60g butter

$3/4$ cup (150g) firmly packed brown sugar

1   Preheat oven to hot. Grease 6-hole texas ($3/4$ cup/180ml) muffin pan.
2   Combine butter, chocolate and sugar in medium saucepan; stir over medium heat until smooth.
3   Stir in egg, essence and flour; divide mixture among muffin pan holes. Cover pan tightly with foil; bake in hot oven about 20 minutes. Remove foil; stand 5 minutes. Place brownies on serving plates; top with ice-cream, caramel sauce and almonds.
    caramel sauce Combine ingredients in small saucepan; stir over medium heat until smooth. Simmer 2 minutes.

serves 6

per serving 44.2g fat; 3164kJ (756 cal)

tip Caramel sauce and the chocolate-melting stage for the brownies can be done in a microwave oven.

waffles and ice-cream à la suzette

PREPARATION TIME 10 MINUTES   COOKING TIME 10 MINUTES

125g butter
½ cup (110g) caster sugar
2 teaspoons finely grated
    orange rind
1 tablespoon orange juice
¼ cup (60ml) Cointreau
8 belgian-style waffles
200ml vanilla ice-cream

1   Melt butter in small heavy-base
     saucepan; add sugar, rind,
     juice and liqueur. Stir over low
     heat, without boiling, until sugar
     dissolves; bring to a boil. Reduce
     heat; simmer, uncovered, without
     stirring, about 1 minute or until
     sauce thickens slightly.
2   Warm waffles according to
     manufacturer's instructions.
     Divide half of the waffles
     among serving plates; top with
     ice-cream, remaining waffles
     and suzette sauce.

serves 4
per serving 41.6g fat;
3012kJ (719 cal)

white chocolate fondue

PREPARATION TIME **10 MINUTES**   COOKING TIME **5 MINUTES**

Traditionally, fondue is served in a single pot that sits in the middle of the table.
Provide your guests with skewers, then watch them dip piece after piece of
fruit or almond bread into the chocolate pot – this will prove a very popular way
to finish the meal! Malibu is the brand name of a rum-based coconut liqueur.

180g white chocolate,
    chopped coarsely
1/2 cup (125ml) cream
1 tablespoon Malibu
1 cup (130g) strawberries
1 large banana (230g),
    chopped coarsely
150g fresh pineapple,
    chopped coarsely
8 slices (35g) almond bread
16 marshmallows (100g)

1   Combine chocolate and cream
    in small saucepan, stir over low
    heat until smooth; stir in liqueur.
    Transfer fondue to serving bowl.
2   Place fondue in centre of
    dining table; serve remaining
    ingredients on a platter.

serves 4
per serving 14.9g fat;
1100kJ (263 cal)
tip Fondue can be served with
any of your favourite fruits.

passionfruit soufflés

PREPARATION TIME 10 MINUTES   COOKING TIME 15 MINUTES

You need four large passionfruit for this recipe.

1 tablespoon caster sugar

2 egg yolks

1/3 cup (80ml) fresh
   passionfruit pulp

2 tablespoons Cointreau

1/2 cup (80g) icing
   sugar mixture

4 egg whites

2 teaspoons icing sugar
   mixture, extra

1   Preheat oven to moderate.
    Lightly grease four 1-cup (250ml)
    ovenproof dishes.

2   Sprinkle insides of dishes evenly
    with caster sugar; shake
    away excess. Place dishes on
    oven tray.

3   Whisk yolks, passionfruit pulp,
    liqueur and 2 tablespoons of the
    icing sugar in large bowl until
    mixture is combined.

4   Beat egg whites in small bowl
    with electric mixer until soft
    peaks form. Gradually add
    remaining icing sugar; beat until
    firm peaks form.

5   Gently fold egg white mixture,
    in two batches, into passionfruit
    mixture; divide mixture among
    prepared dishes.

6   Bake, uncovered, in moderate
    oven about 12 minutes or until
    soufflés are puffed and browned
    lightly. Dust tops with extra sifted
    icing sugar.

serves 4
per serving 2.9g fat;
889kJ (212 cal)
serving suggestion Top with
fresh passionfruit pulp and serve
with cream or ice-cream.

ice-cream timbales with rocky road sauce

PREPARATION TIME **25 MINUTES** COOKING TIME **5 MINUTES**

1 litre (4 cups) vanilla
   ice-cream, softened
2 x 60g Snickers bars,
   chopped finely
2 x 50g Crunchie bars,
   chopped finely
2/3 cup (160ml) thickened cream
100g dark eating chocolate,
   chopped coarsely
100g rocky road,
   chopped coarsely

1 Line four 1-cup (250ml) metal
  moulds with plastic wrap.
2 Place ice-cream in large bowl;
  fold in chocolate bars. Divide
  mixture among prepared moulds.
  Cover with foil; freeze about
  15 minutes or until firm.
3 Meanwhile, heat cream and
  chocolate in small saucepan
  over low heat, stirring until
  smooth. Remove from heat; stir
  rocky road into sauce mixture.
4 Turn ice-cream timbales onto
  serving plates; drizzle with rocky
  road sauce.

serves 4
per serving 51.8g fat;
3544kJ (847 cal)

chocolate rum mini mousse

PREPARATION TIME 10 MINUTES COOKING TIME 5 MINUTES

A variation on the Italian zabaglione, the rum and chocolate transform this into a dessert of great depth and contrasting flavours. Use a Caribbean rum for this recipe, for its mild smooth taste.

6 egg yolks
1/3 cup (75g) caster sugar
1/2 cup (125ml) dark
    rum, warmed
50g dark eating chocolate,
    grated finely

1 Beat egg yolks and sugar in small deep-sided heatproof bowl with electric mixer until light and fluffy.
2 Place bowl over small saucepan of simmering water; whisk egg mixture constantly while gradually adding rum. Continue to whisk until mixture is thick and creamy. Add chocolate, in two batches, whisking gently until chocolate melts between additions.
3 Pour mousse mixture into four 1/3-cup (80ml) serving glasses.

serves 4
per serving 12g fat;
1230kJ (294 cal)
tip The mousse can be served chilled if desired; refrigerate about 2 hours.
serving suggestion Serve with almond biscotti or almond bread.

grilled bananas with malibu syrup

PREPARATION TIME 10 MINUTES   COOKING TIME 5 MINUTES

Malibu is the brand name of a rum-based coconut liqueur.

4 large ripe bananas (920g)
1/3 cup (80ml) maple syrup
2 tablespoons Malibu
1/4 cup (15g) shredded
    coconut, toasted

1   Split bananas lengthways.
    Combine maple syrup and
    liqueur; brush about a quarter
    of the mixture over the cut-sides
    of bananas.
2   Cook bananas, cut-side down,
    on heated lightly oiled grill plate
    (or grill or barbecue) until lightly
    browned and heated through.
3   Serve bananas while hot,
    drizzled with warmed remaining
    syrup and toasted coconut.

serves 4
per serving 2.7g fat;
1122kJ (268 cal)
serving suggestion Serve
bananas with whipped cream and
small glasses of espresso.

chocolate butterscotch tartlets

PREPARATION TIME **5 MINUTES** COOKING TIME **10 MINUTES** (PLUS REFRIGERATION TIME)

12 frozen tartlet cases
¼ cup (55g) firmly packed brown sugar
20g butter
¼ cup (60ml) cream
150g dark eating chocolate, chopped coarsely
¼ cup (60ml) cream, extra
2 tablespoons coarsely chopped roasted hazelnuts
1 tablespoon cocoa powder

1 Bake tartlet cases according to manufacturer's instructions.
2 Meanwhile, heat combined sugar, butter and cream in small saucepan, stirring until sugar dissolves. Reduce heat; simmer, uncovered, without stirring, for 2 minutes. Cool 5 minutes. Stir in chocolate and extra cream; refrigerate 10 minutes.
3 Divide mixture among tartlet cases, sprinkle with nuts and sifted cocoa.

makes 12
per tartlet 38.8g fat; 2352kJ (562 cal)

glossary

almond

FLAKED: paper-thin slices.

MEAL: also known as ground almonds; nuts are powdered to a coarse flour texture, for use in baking or as a thickening agent.

SLIVERED: almonds that have been cut lengthways.

VIENNA: toffee-coated nuts.

amaretti small Italian-style macaroons based on ground almonds.

arrowroot a starch made from the rhizome of a Central American plant, used mostly for thickening. Cornflour can be substituted but will not give as clear a glaze.

bacon rashers also known as slices of bacon, made from pork side, cured and smoked.

baking powder a raising agent consisting mainly of two parts cream of tartar to one part bicarbonate of soda (baking soda).

bean sprouts also known as bean shoots; tender new growths of assorted beans and seeds germinated for consumption in salads and stir-fries.

beans, cannellini small, dried white beans similar in appearance and flavour to other *Phaseolus vulgaris* varieties – great northern and navy or haricot beans.

bicarbonate of soda also known as baking soda.

bok choy also called pak choi or chinese white cabbage; has a fresh, mild mustard taste and is good braised or in stir-fries. Baby bok choy is also available and is slightly more tender than bok choy.

breadcrumbs

PACKAGED: fine-textured, crunchy, purchased, white breadcrumbs.

STALE: one- or two-day-old bread made into crumbs either by grating, blending or processing.

butter use salted or unsalted ("sweet") butter; 125g equals 1 stick butter.

capers the grey-green buds of a warm climate (usually Mediterranean) shrub, sold either dried and salted or pickled in a vinegar brine.

capsicum also known as bell pepper or pepper. Native to Central and South America, it can be red, green, yellow, orange or purplish black. Seeds and membranes should be discarded before use.

caraway seeds a member of the parsley family, sold in seed or ground form.

cardamom native to India and used extensively in its cuisine; can be purchased in pod, seed or ground form. Has a distinctive aromatic, sweetly rich flavour.

cayenne pepper a long, thin-fleshed, extremely hot red chilli; usually purchased dried and ground.

cheese

FETTA: Greek in origin; a crumbly textured goat or sheep milk cheese with a sharp, salty taste.

FONTINA: a smooth firm cheese with a nutty taste and a brown or red rind.

GORGONZOLA: a creamy, cow milk blue cheese. Pierced with needles at about four weeks to encourage the mould to spread; takes about three to six months to fully mature by which time the colour ranges from white to straw yellow with bluish green marbling from the mould.

GRUYÈRE: a Swiss cheese having small holes and a nutty, slightly salty flavour.

HALOUMI: a firm, cream-coloured sheep milk cheese matured in brine; somewhat like a minty, salty fetta in flavour, haloumi can be grilled or fried, briefly, without breaking down.

MASCARPONE: a cultured cream product made in much the same way as yogurt. It's white to creamy yellow in colour, with a soft, creamy texture.

chillies available in many different types and sizes, both fresh and dried. Generally the smaller the chilli, the hotter it is. Use rubber gloves when seeding and chopping fresh chillies as they can burn your skin.

THAI, RED: small, medium hot, and bright red in colour.

chorizo sausage a sausage of Spanish origin, made of coarsely ground pork and highly seasoned with garlic and chillies.

coconut

MILK: pure, unsweetened coconut milk; available in cans and cartons. A lower fat type is also available.

cointreau a clear French orange-flavoured liqueur; 40% alcohol by volume.

coriander also known as cilantro or chinese parsley when fresh; bright green-leafed herb with a pungent flavour. Often stirred into a dish just before serving for maximum impact. Also sold as seeds or ground.

cornflour also known as cornstarch; used as a thickening agent in all types of cooking.

couscous a fine, grain-like cereal product, originally from North Africa; made from semolina.

cream

DOUBLE: (minimum fat content 35%) also known as heavy or whipping cream.

cream of tartar the acid ingredient in baking powder; added to confectionery mixtures to help prevent sugar from crystallising. Keeps frostings creamy and improves volume when beating egg whites.

crème de menthe a mint-flavoured liqueur.

crunchie honeycomb bars coated in chocolate.

cucumber, lebanese short, thin-skinned and slender; this variety is also known as the European or burpless cucumber.

cumin also known as zeera; a spice sold in seed or ground form.

curly endive also known as frisée, a curly-leafed green vegetable, mainly used in salads.

egg some recipes in this book call for raw or barely cooked eggs; exercise caution if there is a salmonella problem in your area.

fish sauce also called nam pla or nuoc nam; made from pulverised salted fermented fish, most often anchovies. Has a pungent smell and strong taste; use sparingly. There are many kinds, of varying intensity.

ginger also known as green or root ginger; the thick gnarled root of a tropical plant. Can be kept, peeled, covered with dry sherry in a jar and refrigerated, or frozen in an airtight container.

hazelnut meal ground hazelnuts.

hoisin sauce a thick, sweet-spicy Chinese paste made from salted fermented soy beans, onions and garlic; used as a marinade or baste, or to accent stir-fries and barbecued foods.

keçap manis also known as ketjap manis; an Indonesian thick soy sauce which has sugar and spices added.

kumara Polynesian name of orange-fleshed sweet potato often confused with yam.

lemon grass a tall, clumping, lemon-smelling and tasting, sharp-edged grass; the white lower part of each stem is chopped and used in Asian cooking or for tea.

malibu brand name of a rum-based coconut liqueur.

marsala a sweet fortified wine originally from Sicily.

mesclun a salad mix of assorted young lettuce and other green leaves, including baby spinach, mizuna and curly endive.

mince meat also known as ground meat.

mirin sweet rice wine used in Japanese cooking; not to be confused with sake, rice wine made for drinking.

mushrooms

SHIITAKE: also sold as donko mushrooms; available fresh and dried. Unique meaty flavour, stronger when dried.

SWISS BROWN: light to dark brown mushrooms with full-bodied flavour, also known as Roman or cremini. Button or cap mushrooms can be substituted.

mustard

AMERICAN: a slightly sweet, mild, bright yellow mustard.

HONEY DIJON: dijon mustard mixed with honey.

SEEDS, BLACK: also known as brown mustard seeds; more pungent than the white (or yellow) seeds used in most prepared mustards.

WHOLEGRAIN: also known as seeded. A French-style coarse-grain mustard made from crushed mustard seeds and dijon-style French mustard.

noodles

FRESH EGG: made from wheat flour and eggs; strands vary in thickness. Used in soups and stir-fries.

HOKKIEN: fresh wheat-flour noodles resembling thick, yellow-brown spaghetti; also known as stir-fry noodles. Rinse under hot water to remove starch and excess oil before use.

RICE STICK: a dried noodle, available flat and wide or very thin; made from rice flour and water.

VERMICELLI: also known as rice-flour noodles and rice-stick noodles. Sold dried, are best either deep-fried or soaked, then stir-fried or used in soups.

nutella an Italian chocolate hazelnut spread.

nutmeg the dried nut of an evergreen tree native to Indonesia; available in ground form or grate your own with a fine grater.

oil

PEANUT: pressed from ground peanuts; most commonly used oil in Asian cooking because of its high smoke point.

SESAME: made from roasted, crushed white sesame seeds. Do not use for frying.

onions, spring vegetables with small white bulbs, long green leaves and narrow green-leafed tops; slightly sweeter than green onions.

pancetta Italian bacon that is cured, but not smoked.

pawpaw also known as papaya or papaw; large, pear-shaped red-orange tropical fruit. Often used unripe (green) in cooking.

pepitas dried pumpkin seeds. Can be purchased salted or unsalted.

pide comes in long (about 45cm) flat loaves as well as individual rounds; made from wheat flour and sprinkled with sesame or black onion seeds.

polenta a flour-like cereal made of ground corn (maize); similar to cornmeal but coarser and darker in colour; also the name of the dish made from it.

prosciutto cured, air-dried (unsmoked), pressed ham; usually sold thinly sliced.

rice

ARBORIO: small, round-grain rice well suited to absorb a large amount of liquid; especially suitable for risottos.

PAPER: an edible, translucent paper made from a dough of water combined with the pith of an Asian shrub called the rice-paper plant (or rice-paper tree).

rocket also known as arugula, rugula and rucola; a peppery-tasting green leaf which can be used in cooking or eaten raw in salad. Baby rocket leaves are smaller and less peppery.

rolled oats whole oat grains that have been steamed and flattened.

rolled rice flattened grain similar to rolled oats.

rolled rye flattened grain similar to rolled oats.

saffron available in strands or ground form; imparts a yellow-orange colour to food once infused. Quality varies greatly; the best is the most expensive spice in the world. Should be stored in the freezer.

sambal oelek (also ulek or olek) Indonesian in origin; a salty paste made from ground chillies.

sambuca a semi-dry Italian liqueur flavoured with anise, herbs, berries, and spices.

snake beans long (about 40cm), thin, round fresh green beans, Asian in origin, with a taste similar to green or french beans. Also called yard-long beans because of their length.

snickers bar made from chocolate, peanuts, sugar, glucose, milk powder, butter and egg white.

soy sauce made from fermented soy beans. Light soy sauce, as the name suggests, is light in colour but generally quite salty. Salt-reduced soy sauce contains less salt.

spinach also known as english spinach and, incorrectly, silverbeet. Tender green leaves are good uncooked in salads or added to soups, stir-fries and stews just before serving. Baby spinach leaves are slightly more tender.

sugar snap peas also known as honey snap peas; snow peas can be substituted.

sumac a purple-red, astringent spice ground from berries growing on shrubs that flourish wild around the Mediterranean. Adds a tart, lemony flavour to dishes.

tandoori paste consisting of garlic, tamarind, ginger, coriander, chilli and spices.

teriyaki sauce homemade or commercially bottled flavouring, made from soy sauce, mirin, sugar, ginger and other spices.

tomato

GRAPE: small, grape-shaped tomatoes similar in texture to cherry tomatoes.

SALSA, BOTTLED: is a combination of tomatoes, onions, peppers, vinegar, herbs and spices.

TEARDROP: small yellow pear-shaped tomatoes.

tortilla thin, round unleavened bread made from corn or wheat; originally from Mexico, can be purchased frozen, fresh or vacuum-packed.

turmeric a member of the ginger family, its root is dried and ground, resulting in the rich yellow powder. It is intensely pungent in taste but not hot.

vanilla essence an inexpensive substitute for pure vanilla extract, made with synthetic vanillin and other flavourings.

vinegar

BALSAMIC: authentic only from the province of Modena, Italy; made from a regional wine of white Trebbiano grapes specially processed, then aged in antique wooden casks to give an exquisite pungent flavour.

CIDER: made from fermented apples.

RICE: made from fermented rice, colourless and flavoured with sugar and salt. Also known as seasoned rice vinegar.

wasabi an Asian horseradish used to make the pungent, green-coloured sauce traditionally served with Japanese raw fish dishes; sold in powdered or paste form.

witlof also known as chicory or belgian endive.

worcestershire sauce a thin, dark-brown spicy sauce used as a seasoning and condiment.

zucchini also known as courgette, belonging to the squash family.

conversion chart

measures

One Australian metric measuring cup holds approximately 250ml, one Australian metric tablespoon holds 20ml, one Australian metric teaspoon holds 5ml.

The difference between one country's measuring cups and another's is within a two- or three-teaspoon variance, and will not affect your cooking results. North America, New Zealand and the United Kingdom use a 15ml tablespoon.

All cup and spoon measurements are level. The most accurate way of measuring dry ingredients is to weigh them. When measuring liquids, use a clear glass or plastic jug with the metric markings.

We use large eggs with an average weight of 60g.

dry measures

METRIC	IMPERIAL
15g	½oz
30g	1oz
60g	2oz
90g	3oz
125g	4oz (¼lb)
155g	5oz
185g	6oz
220g	7oz
250g	8oz (½lb)
280g	9oz
315g	10oz
345g	11oz
375g	12oz (¾lb)
410g	13oz
440g	14oz
470g	15oz
500g	16oz (1lb)
750g	24oz (1½lb)
1kg	32oz (2lb)

liquid measures

METRIC	IMPERIAL
30ml	1 fluid oz
60ml	2 fluid oz
100ml	3 fluid oz
125ml	4 fluid oz
150ml	5 fluid oz (¼ pint/1 gill)
190ml	6 fluid oz
250ml	8 fluid oz
300ml	10 fluid oz (½ pint)
500ml	16 fluid oz
600ml	20 fluid oz (1 pint)
1000ml (1 litre)	1¾ pints

length measures

METRIC	IMPERIAL
3mm	⅛in
6mm	¼in
1cm	½in
2cm	¾in
2.5cm	1in
5cm	2in
6cm	2½in
8cm	3in
10cm	4in
13cm	5in
15cm	6in
18cm	7in
20cm	8in
23cm	9in
25cm	10in
28cm	11in
30cm	12in (1ft)

oven temperatures

These oven temperatures are only a guide for conventional ovens. For fan-forced ovens, check the manufacturer's manual.

	°C (CELSIUS)	°F (FAHRENHEIT)	GAS MARK
Very slow	120	250	½
Slow	150	275-300	1-2
Moderately slow	160	325	3
Moderate	180	350-375	4-5
Moderately hot	200	400	6
Hot	220	425-450	7-8
Very hot	240	475	9

index

ARE YOU MISSING SOME OF THE WORLD'S FAVOURITE COOKBOOKS?

The Australian Women's Weekly Cookbooks are available from bookshops, cookshops, supermarkets and other stores all over the world. You can also buy direct from the publisher, using the order form below.

TITLE	RRP	QTY	TITLE	RRP	QTY
Asian Meals in Minutes	£6.99		Great Lamb Cookbook	£6.99	
Babies & Toddlers Good Food	£6.99		Greek Cooking Class	£6.99	
Barbecue Meals In Minutes	£6.99		Healthy Heart Cookbook	£6.99	
Basic Cooking Class	£6.99		Indian Cooking Class	£6.99	
Beginners Cooking Class	£6.99		Japanese Cooking Class	£6.99	
Beginners Simple Meals	£6.99		Kids' Birthday Cakes	£6.99	
Beginners Thai	£6.99		Kids Cooking	£6.99	
Best Food	£6.99		Lean Food	£6.99	
Best Food Desserts	£6.99		Low-carb, Low-fat	£6.99	
Best Food Fast	£6.99		Low-fat Feasts	£6.99	
Best Food Mains	£6.99		Low-fat Food For Life	£6.99	
Cakes, Biscuits & Slices	£6.99		Low-fat Meals in Minutes	£6.99	
Cakes Cooking Class	£6.99		Main Course Salads	£6.99	
Caribbean Cooking	£6.99		Middle Eastern Cooking Class	£6.99	
Casseroles	£6.99		Midweek Meals in Minutes	£6.99	
Chicken	£6.99		Muffins, Scones & Breads	£6.99	
Chicken Meals in Minutes	£6.99		New Casseroles	£6.99	
Chinese Cooking Class	£6.99		New Classics	£6.99	
Christmas Cooking	£6.99		New Finger Food	£6.99	
Chocolate	£6.99		Party Food and Drink	£6.99	
Cocktails	£6.99		Pasta Meals in Minutes	£6.99	
Cooking for Friends	£6.99		Potatoes	£6.99	
Creative Cooking on a Budget	£6.99		Salads: Simple, Fast & Fresh	£6.99	
Detox	£6.99		Saucery	£6.99	
Dinner Beef	£6.99		Sauces, Salsas & Dressings	£6.99	
Dinner Lamb	£6.99		Sensational Stir-Fries	£6.99	
Dinner Seafood	£6.99		Short-order Cook	£6.99	
Easy Australian Style	£6.99		Slim	£6.99	
Easy Curry	£6.99		Sweet Old-fashioned Favourites	£6.99	
Easy Spanish-style Cookery	£6.99		Thai Cooking Class	£6.99	
Essential Soup	£6.99		Vegetarian Meals in Minutes	£6.99	
Freezer, Meals from the	£6.99		Vegie Food	£6.99	
French Food, New	£6.99		Weekend Cook	£6.99	
Fresh Food for Babies & Toddlers	£6.99		Wicked Sweet Indulgences	£6.99	
Get Real, Make a Meal	£6.99		Wok Meals in Minutes	£6.99	
Good Food Fast	£6.99		TOTAL COST:	£	

Mr/Mrs/Ms _____

Address _____

_____ Postcode _____

Day time phone _____ Email* (optional) _____

I enclose my cheque/money order for £ _____

or please charge £ _____

to my: ☐ Access   ☐ Mastercard   ☐ Visa   ☐ Diners Club

PLEASE NOTE: WE DO NOT ACCEPT SWITCH OR ELECTRON CARDS

Card number ☐☐☐☐☐☐☐☐☐☐☐☐☐☐☐☐

Expiry date _____ 3 digit security code *(found on reverse of card)* _____

Cardholder's name_____ Signature _____

* By including your email address, you consent to receipt of any email regarding this magazine, and other emails which inform you of ACP's other publications, products, services and events, and to promote third party goods and services you may be interested in.

To order: Mail or fax – photocopy or complete the order form above, and send your credit card details or cheque payable to: Australian Consolidated Press (UK), Moulton Park Business Centre, Red House Road, Moulton Park, Northampton NN3 6AQ, phone (+44) (0) 1604 497531 fax (+44) (0) 1604 497533, e-mail books@acpmedia.co.uk or order online at www.acpuk.com
Non-UK residents: We accept the credit cards listed on the coupon, or cheques, drafts or International Money Orders payable in sterling and drawn on a UK bank. Credit card charges are at the exchange rate current at the time of payment.
Postage and packing UK: Add £1.00 per order plus 50p per book.
Postage and packing overseas: Add £2.00 per order plus £1.00 per book.
All pricing current at time of going to press and subject to change/availability.
Offer ends 31.12.2007